Eva Luz

by
Barro

Order this book online at www.trafford.com
or email orders@trafford.com

Most Trafford titles are also available at major online book retailers.

Printed in Victoria, BC, Canada.

ISBN: 978-1-4251-3944-5 (Soft)
ISBN: 978-1-4251-8893-1 (e-book)

*Our mission is to efficiently provide the world's finest, most comprehensive
book publishing service, enabling every author to experience success.
To find out how to publish your book, your way, and have it available
worldwide, visit us online at www.trafford.com*

Trafford rev. 01/05/2010

 www.trafford.com

North America & international
toll-free: 1 888 232 4444 (USA & Canada)
phone: 250 383 6864 ♦ fax: 812 355 4082

Contents

The Daisy Seller

I'm so tired of fighting with everything, with the others, with the world, with myself. Life weighs down on me… I weigh myself down. What am I doing here? This isn't my place. I feel awful, upset, surrounded by so many people… and so alone.

I'm falling asleep. I feel like vomiting and I'm dizzy. The loudspeakers shake every cell in my body. What a scene! A fantastic party. Mixing so many shitty drinks has left me feeling terrible. I'm sad, unfortunate. My self-esteem is very low.

Staying with the group isn't doing me any good. I should have left them a long time ago. When I met them I was attracted to their dynamics, their careless manners, their cheerful, happy, uninhibited ways…

I thought it would be therapeutic to be with them, that they would help me to overcome or reduce my states of isolation and sadness. I thought they would cheer me up, ignite my desire to live and my low level of enthusiasm. At first this is how it was, but as time passed problems and incompatibilities arose. Now they hurt me. When I was surrounded by solitude I took refuge in them, hoping they would alleviate it. They were mirages. In general, their criticisms, jokes and rejections brought me down even further.

Their way of having a good time, the places they went to, like the one tonight, used to cheer me up, but now I find them difficult. I'm fed up. I find them frivolous and superficial. These places make our differences stand out, separating us even more.

If I'm tired with this place, if it's not for me, why don't I leave? That's easy, because I can hardly stand up. I'm wrecked. Plus, if they stop me and make me do a breathalyzer, it'll be positive. Plus,

I don't have money to pay for the ticket, they would probably take away my licence. All of these things discourage and immobilize me.

I'm tired of chasing them, of always being left behind. It's not their fault. I'm somewhere I shouldn't be. I have to choose my own paths. I shouldn't ally myself with troubadours when I like jazz and I shouldn't sign-up for others' plans when I don't even like or enjoy them.

I have to decide, once and for all, to find my own path and start following it, and to substitute the cabin boy that scrubs the deck for my inner warrior full of strength.

Feelings of loneliness, lack of affection and abandonment unsettle my life. It emotionally overwhelms me with sorrows and tears. It exhausts me mentally and physically, depresses me and embitters my life. It's those feelings that have brought me here, seeking the group's companionship.

Sorrows, where do you come from? I'm so fed up with you. You haunt me. You're always ready to ruin my happy moments, my desire to live. I don't want to see you anymore. I rebel against my helplessness to rid myself of you. Every time I brush you off you instantly come back, like a persistent fly.

I vehemently want to free myself from you, to send you into the next black hole. But you're ethereal, inapprehensible. You tip-toe furtively, taking my energy, mood, happiness away... Enough already! Get away from me. Disappear. You're dormant for a time, and suddenly, you erupt like lava from a volcano but with more force.

I try to flee from you, faking festive, high emotional states, but I don't deceive anybody, myself included. I want to be a bird's song instead of a hired sorrowful mourner.

Are you good for anything, besides upsetting and mortifying me? Are you purifying me in some way? Do you make me better, stronger, more conscious, tolerant or human? Are you settling some old debt? Ani once told me: "Eva, it's likely that your feeling of neglect and abandonment comes from some unresolved matter from a past life. Maybe you received a harsh rejection, lack of love or esteem from someone, that made you feel unappreciated, marginalized, unloved, like an outsider. Perhaps that lack of love was indelibly marked in your historical memory by a painful solitude that still remains. On the other hand, maybe you hurt someone, which made you, besides having an inferiority complex, also feel guilty. It's not surprising that with these emotional states there are moments when you feel awful. When you discover where and how this lack of love was born, it's likely that all of your misfortune will disappear like a cloud. Be aware of what life brings to your shores: your dreams, your memories, your state of mind, the people and situations that life presents to you. There could be clues that you need to remember.

Keep in mind the importance of meditation. It'll help you find the answers you need. Maybe, chasing after the love that you never received, unconsciously, is the reason why you're always in a hurry and sad, and why you go begging for crumbs of esteem."

I think Ani's right: that I still carry this weight in my heart, running after others, with the imperative need to receive their positive evaluations, to prove to myself that I'm worth something and that I'm appreciated.

When I'm not on the brink of tears I'm a different person. My contained happiness explodes. I sing, laugh, dance, make plans and get excited. I'm practically unrecognizable. I've got a great desire to live. I'm like a bird that finds its cage door open. I think this attitude represents my real personality, the Inner Me.

Here comes the "flirt" of the group. She's going to say: "Hi, Cinderella" to me, which bothers me a lot.

"Hi, Cinderella. You look sad. It looks like you were at your five o'clock prayer. You should live in a hermitage. You're hopeless. I need you to give me a hand."

I'm fed up with the group's comparisons. Ben was the first one to start it, and everyone else did it too when they saw how their criticisms annoyed me.

"Do you see that good-looking guy at the bar? The one who's talking with the guy that has a billard ball-like head? I'm going to go over there. How much do you want to bet that in less than three minutes I'll captivate him?"

"Nothing. I don't gamble."

"Listen carefully I'm going to tell you the plan. I´ll go over and dazzle him with my charm and wit. When you see me touch my necklace, come over and hand me the cell phone saying, 'Excuse me boss, the network's calling, it's important.' Then I'll say, 'Tell them I'm in a meeting and that I'll call them back later.' Do you get it? It will make me look important."

"Look, sorry, I'm going to pass on your little show, I feel a bit dizzy."

"That's what I thought, I can't count on you for anything. You're living in the Middle Ages. I'll manage better without you, because with your appearance and your depressing air you might just ruin my plan anyway. You're useless!"

What a rude way of treating people, so humiliating, always undervaluing and rubbing my emotions in my face. I've asked her to stop many times, but she doesn't listen, the problem is that the rest of the group behaves the same way. I can't stand them anymore. In the beginning they weren't so unfriendly. I sense that tonight will be the last time that I go out with them.

"Here I go. Watch closely and enjoy my brilliance. Watch how he falls captive at my feet."

She heads toward them with an air of arrogance. They're talking animatedly and she interrupts them without any consideration. They carry on talking as if nothing has happened. They don't even look at her, ignoring her as if she were invisible. What a snub! Now, the good-looking one with an angry face turns around and tells her something. She runs off. She's coming this way. I can hardly keep myself from laughing, having seen her demonstrate her talent.

"I don't want a single comment. And you can wipe that grin off your face! A well-timed retreat is a victory too. They're incompetent and unbearable assholes. Football has made them stupid. The cute jerk said: 'Can't you see that you're bothering us? Get out of here.' Guys aren't what they used to be. Nothing is like it used to be. They've lost their passionate sides… maybe it's caused by all the pollution."

"Don't worry about it. The night's young."

"Of course, I'm going to take another look around. It's not so easy to curb my enthusiasm. It's his loss, ,."

Tonight I am feeling down. Nostalgia and melancholy surround my soul. I don't know where they come from but can only feel their symptoms: depression and tears pushed out by a deep, inner sadness. These feelings have kept me with the group and what good has it done me? Well, everything is good for something. At least they've helped me figure out that I have to find solutions to my problems by myself. They're my personal lessons.

Tonight would be like any other night with the group: attacks and counterattacks and pointless exhibitionisms along with the unbearably loud beat of the music. But it's causing a significant reaction in me. My inner warrior is waking up: "Enough! Eva, use your time wisely, don't waste it, don't give it away! It's the most precious thing you have. Don't give up your power!"

Okay! I'm leaving the group! This time it's for real. Every day we're more out of tune with each other and we get along worse and worse. They remind me of baby animals, half of the time playing and the other half fighting, always testing their strength.

The group's roadrunner is coming this way, trotting, pushing her way across the dance floor. She'll say a bunch of swear words at me. At first, I told her to shut up, but this only added fuel to her fire. Now, I let her criticize me. I ignore her criticisms by using the silent treatment, it's that simple. I become mute. I use the same tactic with the rest of the group. They provoke me, but I don't respond. That way I don't get hooked in and I save energy.

Not getting angry or confronting those that are looking for a fight leaves them powerless to irritate me. I think that their offences are directed at another person, so I don't counterattack.

This defence mechanism helps make them aware of their attitude and moderate it rather than increase it.

"What are you doing here standing so quietly? You look sick. Do you have any perfume? I smell horribly of sweat, the dance floor is like a sauna and I've been dancing all night. You look like one of those living street statues. I wouldn't be surprised if someone threw some change to see your show. My ex-boyfriend is here, when he finds me he's going to bombard me with questions. I want to impress him. I wouldn't mind getting back together with him. Can you give me the perfume?"

"I don't wear any."

"Oh, right… Does this purse belong to someone in the group?"

"Yes, she's dancing."

"Let's see if I have any luck and I find a perfume spray. It looks like a suitcase. What a disaster! She has all of her stuff in here, all she's missing are the flowerpots. Aha! Here it is. I'll put on a little drop on my neck… Nothing's coming out, I'll press it harder… Nothing, I'll try screwing off the top. I can't see it in this light. Shit! What a mess! The top has come off and now there's a river of perfume down my cleavage all the way down to my hips. The cap is stuck in my dress waist. Fuck, I reek of perfume. I practically need a mask. The cap is sliding around like a fish. What must people think I'm looking for? Ah, I've got it. Is the smell that noticeable?"

"Do you need to ask? It's overwhelming. The smell of your sweat was more bearable and natural. This stench will open a path for you everywhere you go." I'm cracking up! Perfume down to her hips! It'll take months to get rid of the smell… not even a hose could get rid of it. It smells like garlic.

"Did you read the label? Are you sure that it's perfume? Let's see… It's an extract made out of garlic juice to season food!"

"Shit, just what I needed! I hate the fucking smell of garlic. Why do they make the fucking extract's bottle so small and pretty? I smell like an onion hamburger! It probably has fucking onion extract, too. I'm going to the bathroom to see if scrubbing it will make it go away."

"If you don't mind, can you take the bottle?" Unless she's using a scouring pad...

"I'm going to try to avoid my ex-boyfriend."

"Good luck."

"Hi! Do you want to buy some flowers? Come on, I'm going home and I'm really tired. Buy these last few flowers that I have left."

"Hello. Everyone else sells roses or carnations. How come you sell daisies?"

"It's your favorite flower, right?"

"Yes, how do you know?"

"I know."

"I don't have any money left."

"It doesn't matter, accept them as a gift."

"Why are you giving them to me?"

"I don't know, maybe because you're a precious being and you deserve them."

"Wow, thank you. But there are too many just for me."

"You can give them to your friends. It'll be a nice farewell gift."

"Thank you, daisy seller."

"Good luck honey."

What a magical encounter! What a special person! I had never seen her around here. I was about to ask her how she knew about the farewell... but she would have said, "I know."

They're playing my song! It goes directly to my heart, its musical notes pushing me toward the dance floor. The night has changed color. The fairies are sprinkling their golden stars. I'm not dizzy anymore.

I'm going to dance. On the dance floor, almost everyone dances without a partner. I'll dance alone. I'll leave everything behind and let the music take me away... It reminds me of a rainy afternoon, of a ship heading out to sea, of temporal, remote things...

This music makes my romantic fiber vibrate. It intoxicates me. It raises my spirit. Its spell transports me. It moves my heart, elevates my spirit. It has strength. It sounds like an epic. It evokes an image of a group of people heading out on an epic mission, getting closer and closer to their destiny… Getting closer! These words remind me of the phrase I heard in my dream last night. It's been with me since then, caressing me. Its fragrance has been following me all day. It was short, but it left a lasting impression on me, I remember it very well:

I found myself in a space full of radiant white light. I felt like I was part of the light. Within the light there appeared a pair of beautiful eyes, their deep look radiating an indescribable love. Their energy caressed me, filled me with emotion. The eyes were familiar… As they came closer, I felt a sudden happiness, fullness… and then I heard, "We're getting closer, my love." Its voice made me vibrate intensely, filling me with love and peace… I woke up crying, with tears of immeasurable happiness. My song has ended. I return to the table. The dance floor has suddenly become crowded. Okay, I'm going to hand out the daisies.

Mission accomplished, everyone in the group has received their daisy. Now it's Ben's turn. The daisy will be my symbol of love and friendship. A peace offering. I don't want to leave any matter unresolved with anybody in the group. I'll offer it to him with a smile on my face and love in my heart. Here I go… He's sitting with his legs splayed out on his throne, omnipotent.

He knows that I'm standing here but he doesn't deign to look at me. He continues playing the part of the king of rejection. I hold out my hand, offering him the daisy. My conciliatory gesture of understanding and forgiveness. My arm is going to get tired. He doesn't lift a single finger. He continues ignoring me as if I don't exist. He maintains his armor of bitterness and hostility. Scornful, offensive and condescending. He doesn't know, he doesn't answer. I've handed him an opportunity to show me his arrogance on a silver platter, and he's taking advantage of it. He's enjoying it.

That's enough. I'll leave the daisy on the table with my best wishes, without any resentment for his lack of consideration.

In the beginning I liked Ben a lot, but I was wrong about him. The admiration that the group had toward him influenced me a lot. I idealized him, put him on a pedestal, something I shouldn't do with anybody. I felt drawn to him, but then, as I got to know him my fascination diminished. I realized that his manners lacked any brightness of feeling. They appeared weak, empty. He is like a book filled with blank pages but with a beautiful cover.

He realized it and started with his old conquering tricks. His reputation was at stake. His moves were failing him, one after another, and he got angry with me. He turned our relationship into an arm wrestling match, to see who was the strongest. Relationships are difficult. Nobody possesses anybody. It's important to live and let live, and to allow everyone to follow their own path. We should all wear that on t-shirts.

There was a point when his scorn, his arrogance and his silence affected me. All the girls went after him. He was a show off. He was always strutting around, showing off his beautiful peacock feathers. But I was missing from his collection of trophies. This hurt him. It was a hard blow to his self-esteem, to his spoiled ego. He doesn't like to lose. This whole time he's been resentful toward me.

He hasn't given up yet. He has persistently continued trying all of his conquering techniques, not quitting until he has collected the last sticker for his album. He hasn't gotten the result he was looking for, because he keeps forgetting to join his root chakra to the one in his heart.

He's used to sneaking-up on girls with his bag of seduction tricks on his back. But you can see him coming a mile away. Do you know why your tricks don't work? They're all missing one ingredient, the spice of life: Love. You've got it bottled up inside, held captive. You're also missing another ingredient: authenticity. You have a calculating mind, crouched, ready to pounce. You're obsessed with quick conquest manuals that limit you from seeing the big picture.

You walk around looking distant with your hands in your pockets, with the object of your desire in front of you, looking distracted, uninterested. Like a pigeon after its mate. From your stuffed back pocket I can see another manual, you're overloaded! It's called "How to Seduce a Girl on the First Date." It's outdated and hasn't been upgraded.

The manuals haven't worked on me because they don't have feelings. If you were honest, you wouldn't need the books. You've forgotten the tactics of the heart. You can't replace or improvise them. They come out when your heart is awake, alive, not sleeping, snoring. You have to use it so that it can grow.

I need a relationship that won't hurt me, it has to involve respect, tenderness and love. Your power and magnetism over me has vanished. I'm sorry, but it wasn't up to me. It's my heart that decides at that level.

Ben's doing his thing, he's weaving my daisy into a foreign girl's hair at the next table. The last sparks of affection I felt for him when I first met him disappear behind the flower petals.

The rebuffs, rejections, gestures of repulsion and hostility hurt me even though it doesn't look like it. I dance on the outside and cry on the inside. My feelings perceive them from far away, even though they're wrapped in colored tissue paper and perfumed with fine irony. For him, it's a game, for me it's not. His hostility intensifies the solitude that sleeps within me. His rejections are recorded in my heart and leave a trail of sadness, which takes a long time to go away.

He watches me out of the corner of his eye, checking to see what impact his action has caused. Tonight it doesn't affect me. It's my goodbye. The foreign girl gets up and hugs a friend that has just arrived. She ignores Ben and leaves without looking at him. She's left the daisy on the table. His conquering ego probably didn't take too kindly to the rejection.

He gets up and moves toward me. Oops, he tripped. He's a little drunk and looks very irritated. The girl's contempt toward him has made him feel awful.

"Hi, Ben. What brings you here?"

"Let's dance."

"No, thanks. Let me go! Those are some manners you've got." When the girl went off with her friend, she brought Ben's nastiness and arrogance to the surface.

"Your loss. Give me the car keys. I'm going to town to get something to eat."

"Denied."

"You're exasperating, the most unbearable one of the group. Always making problems, always negative. You won't give me the keys because you think I'll crash the car. You're fucking uptight."

"Six months ago, you broke my headlight when you crashed into a streetlight, and I'm still waiting for you to pay me back, as you promised. And please watch your language."

"Don't keep me waiting. Give me the keys."

"Forget about me. Get lost! Get out of here!"

He turns around and moves away, stumbling, in a very bad mood, furious. The group is going from bad to worse. Before they were more presentable. I think Ben's attitude is making things worse. It's a pity that he's the one who everyone follows and that he doesn't open doors to other possibilities.

I'm leaving. I'm physically exhausted. Where's everyone? Whatever, I already said goodbye with the daisies...

What a cool breeze! It's so refreshing. There's part of the group. Shit! They've seen me. They're coming over here. I'll take out the car keys and see if I can get in before they get here.

"Hey! Wait! Give us a ride to town. We're starving."

"Sorry, I'm going home. It's already four... Hey, Ben! Give me back my keys. You hurt my hand when you grabbed them."

"Forget about it. You can get as angry as you want."

"You're not all thinking about getting in? It's against the law."

"Quick, get in this crappy car. Let's see what it can really do. Goodbye, countess. We're leaving you here. See you later."

If I don't hurry up, they'll leave without me. I hardly fit, it's full. He's started-up the car. Half of my body is outside. He makes a violent turn. I practically fall out. He's pretty drunk and he's putting us in real danger. I feel like I'm going to throw up. I'll do it out the window.

It's a good thing we're almost there. He's driven up on the curb and he's lost control of the steering wheel!

"Look out for that line of trees, you're going to run into them! Brake now! Watch out for the trees! Brake, brake! Slow down! Watch out... the trees! Brake, brake!" The poor car is getting scratched up. It'll only be fit for the junk yard.

"Everybody out. We're at the bar. Door to door service. It couldn't have been done any better. They've got legendary sandwiches."

Everyone jumps out, eager to touch solid ground. The keys are in the ignition! I'll take advantage of the confusion to get them. Okay, I'm in control. I'll lock the doors. Ben's seen my maneuver and comes running.

"Hey! What are you doing? Get out of the car."

He's trying to open the doors. Finding them locked pisses him off. He starts taking out his anger on the car, kicking and punching it. The others are watching the spectacle and complain because I'm leaving them without a car.

"You're not going to leave us stranded here, are you?"

"No problem. Call a taxi. It's not my responsibility. This is my last night. I'm sorry that everything's so messed up. Life has brought us together. There must have been some reason for it. Thank you all for having been a mirror for me, for showing me what I have to discard and what I have to improve in myself. And thank you even more for making me conscious of the sparkles I carry in my backpack of stars. Good luck, I love you all."

"You'll be back, you always come back."

"Not this time. My inner warrior has woken up. She's risen up and activated my strength. Thank you for sharing your wisdom with me… in your own way. Have a nice life."

Heavens! What a relief! I'm finally alone. It's a good thing the car works. "My pretty car, try to resist how badly the group has treated you tonight and make an effort to get me home."

Good, the end of an era. It's time to get away from them. I've tried to appeal to their hearts several times, and they've continued to keep them locked, stepping all over my principles. We've learned the lessons that we had to go through together. Our relationship has helped us grow. Now I have to change the record.

Sometimes I've judged them, forgetting that in their hearts beats the same Light that we all have inside, which I have too. Behind their rudeness their Light beats. Behind their egoistic competitions their Light beats. Behind their superficial chatter loaded with false intentions their Light beats. Behind their acidic and scornful mocking humor their Light beats… and as they walk it will become brighter until they transform themselves into radiant and luminous lighthouses.

Now is the beginning of another journey. It's a time of change, of expanding my horizons. I'm excited to face the challenges that, in part, I neglected because I dedicated that time and money to the group…

The Era of the "Clickers"

It's good to come back at this hour because I don't have to see the doorman's face. I can't stand him. I'm aware that it's another opportunity that life gives me to practice my humility and tolerance.

My stomach is churning. I don't know if I'll be able to make it to the bathroom. I don't even want to think about it. My poor body, I make you work so hard because I don't take care of you. I treat you badly. I've had you running on nothing but liquids all night long and I haven't offered you anything solid. We're going on to the second day of an involuntary fast, forced upon us by an empty bank account. You, my poor stomach, diplomatically murmur your displeasures. Your suppressed complaints throw my poor economic sense in my face. It doesn't do you any good. If there's no water, you can't drink.

Where the hell are the keys? This isn't a purse, it's a trunk. Did I leave them inside the apartment? I don't want to think about it, I'm always in a hurry. Here they are right at the bottom! Now, race to the finish line, or I won't arrive on time. Faster, faster! Sit down. What a wonderful throne of kings and queens! It sounds like an orchestra. What a relief!

Oh, no! There's no water in the tank. They've cut me off again for not paying the bills. I'll have to go down to the fountain and fill some pitchers to get rid of this smell.

Wow! Look at those bags under my eyes, I look wrecked. I'll have to cover the mirror…

Shit, the elevator's jerking its way down and the door's shaking. Don't fail me now, make it to the lobby. I don't feel like being locked in here all night. Wouldn't that be the highlight of this great party! Thank goodness, it's gone down all the way! The door's half-open. I don't fit. I'll empty my lungs. Whew, I barely made it!

The street is deserted. Everybody's settling down in their beds. It's the best time to carry water. No gossiping neighbors. No teasing doorman.

My eyes won't stay open, I'm falling asleep holding on to the faucet. A cold breeze is rising and I'm still wearing my sheer party clothes. I'm freezing…

They're so heavy, eight liters on each arm, I'm going to get monkey arms. I'll skip the elevator. I don't feel like getting trapped between floors for the rest of the night.

I'm only at the fifth floor and I'm panting, I can't take it anymore. I'm really out of shape. My legs can't take it. I'll sit down and catch my breath.

I'm getting too sleepy. The last thing I need is to fall asleep on the landing. The odious doorman will be happy to find me here in the morning, next to the water bottles, curled-up and snoring. His cynical and mocking comments piss me off, like: "Good morning, Miss Eva. Visiting the fountain, again? You're wasting public water that all citizens pay for, that I pay for…"

I don't understand him. When he makes me angry I react indignantly yet he still responds with a satisfied expression on his face…

I'll ration it out, I'll pour the smallest possible amount. Precious liquid, water that cleans and dilutes. Goodbye, smell. And, without wasting any more time, I'm off to bed.

At last! I gently let myself fall… I've actually fallen really heavily, I almost broke the bed. I'm wrecked. I won't turn on the alarm clock. My dear body, sleep… until you recov… er…

from all… of this… I… I… love… you…ve…ve…very…very… much…

Where am I? It sounds like the house is collapsing! What a racket! It's eight o'clock! I've only slept two hours… It's the neighbor's little angel, working on his toy carpenter's bench. He's having a great time banging on it. His mother has placed her noise factory right next to our common wall. She has a problem with me. What a bunch of great neighbors!

It's impossible for anyone to sleep in these conditions. Every person's freedom ends where the next person's begins. I'm hungry. Let's see if I can find something to eat. Eating something will calm down my bad mood, brought on by the banging.

It's freezing in here. Without water, the heating doesn't work. The apartment is like an igloo. I'll solve the problem by putting on layers of socks, sweaters and gloves. It's very uncomfortable. If I were a bear, I wouldn't need all this, not even with temperatures as low as fifty below zero. I miss good weather. When it's cold I'm nobody, I get sluggish.

I'll dig through all the cupboards for some lost delicacy. What a pathetic lack of food. A cookie! No, it's a lid from a jar of olives, witness to a time of abundance. A rotten onion. What a stench! An egg box full of air. A pine nut! I'll make it last until I transform it into a sorbet, by passing it back and forth in my mouth. Yum, it tastes so good. In its glory years, this cupboard must have been a rich deposit of dried fruit. Thank you grandma for your legacy. You got me used to adding a dose of humor to difficult situations.

Economic shortages have made me fast a lot, leading to the transformation of all saleable items into bread, oil and onion. The refrigerator, stereo, digital camera, television, laptop… have all fallen, sold second-hand to the highest bidder to sate the hunger of my genuine and demanding stomach. The apartment has begun to take on a spacious look, like a desert steppe. Visitors, of which I have less and less, ask me if I'm moving. I buy brand new things and then, when I'm broke and starving, I sell them at rock-bottom prices. And on those few occasions when I have some money left over, I replace them. It's a disastrous system. That was before. I no longer replace things. I've gotten used to living day-to-day, caravan-style with hardly any objects or belongings... travelling light.

Having no money has simplified my life, making it less complicated. It's done away with habits and junk that required unnecessary obligations. I'll try and make sure that the new changes don't take up my time, but free it. The more things you have, the more fixing, dusting, washing and organizing you do. They waste time and space.

More and more, my acquaintances have stopped coming to visit me. To be comfortable, they need to be near an image or a sound-producing machine: the TV, laptop, radio, stereo... and they don't find such amusements here.

When my guests go into the kitchen looking for something to nibble on and exercise their jawbones, they're shocked when they don't find a refrigerator. They miss it. I understand, it happens to me too, even though I'm used to it.

They unconsciously believe that the food coffer, just like the image box, can't be missing, that it must be somewhere waiting for them with its tempting song: "Come, discover my hidden treasures."

Sitting or stretching out on the floor cracks their knee and back joints. They miss their comfy armchairs. They've forgotten that sharing their epic deeds, exploits and their wisdom around the campfire sparks and crackles the emotion in their hearts and intensifies their self-satisfaction.

If they aren't surrounded by digital gadgets, they don't feel complete. They've transformed themselves into passive receptors of news that, in general, doesn't concern them. They're losing the habit of coming up with their own ideas, newly born from their emotions, feelings and creativity. They don't appreciate them, consider them important, interesting, or worthy of attention compared with the pre-packaged ones that they get from the media...

In the future, historians studying this time will drive themselves crazy trying to understand why the people developed a disproportionately long index finger on their right hand, and why the size of their rear end increased so much. Until a smart and clever paleontologist solves the mystery. He'll name them the marvelous human "button clickers." The era of the clickers.

I also succumbed to the hook. I transformed myself into a compulsive consumer of images, an addicted button clicker of remote controls. The only thing I needed to be completely happy was a folding chair attached to my ass. I wasn't able to control myself. I came home tired, collapsed on the sofa, and started to click buttons. Sleepy, stretched out, languishing... I clicked, I'd watch everything: commercials, the weather, sports, cooking shows, boring movies, gossip about famous people... Desiring the greatness behind the screen... languished I'd click...

I was fascinated by the parade of desires that appeared before me. Things I had never thought about, that I didn't need, but, without which, according to the screen, I would never be happy. I ran after them, but when I had them I realized that my happiness, the real one, hadn't increased, it had actually diminished because the wish list transferred to my mental agenda was so implausible that it actually weighed me down.

I wasn't strong enough to break free from it. It subjugated me. I'd surf from one channel to the next looking for a program that would satisfy me. I couldn't find it because it wasn't on the screen. It was right in front of it, in me, in my heart. The remote control would need to have a new button that would connect me with the stellar program, created and directed by me. The button could be inscribed with: This is the magic button. If you press it, with the practice of meditation, it will be activated and will take you directly to your heart, to the joy of living, to fullness, to your Inner Wisdom.

Life, disguised as poverty, gave me a hand. Images or sandwiches... I sold the image-producing machines. It was a blessing. They ceased stealing my time and money when they stopped overflowing my schedule with activities and obligations. Goodbye to always going at full speed, to the despair of having, wanting and needing to be everywhere, doing, seeing and talking about everything, knowing the latest about everything... but not about myself.

Now I can get my ass off the chair and get into gear. I have regained my power, which had been stuck to the button of the remote. Now, I'm the main character, the creator, the dancer, the poet, the singer, the beggar, the painter, the clown, the writer, the adventurer, someone with a real taste for life.

However, I have to admit that the media: the TV, radio, Internet, movies, books... is either an evolutionary or an impoverishing tool. Two key words establish its position: The first one is Choice, knowing how to choose the best programs, the beautiful and enriching ones, created from the heart with imagination and inspiration. And the second one is Moderation, all things in appropriate amounts. Knowing how to detach myself from the remote control and not become an insatiable consumer of pre-packaged images, sounds and words, helps me to create a balanced equilibrium between contemplation and action. Otherwise I would become more passive and live everyone else's lives, instead of my own.

I've just had a good idea. I'll change the movies that I don't like for a 3-D movie with all the color and the latest special effects. It'll be very realistic, with believable and normal characters, just like in real life. Bring up the backdrop, the title reads: *Eva, Her Adventures and Miracles.* My movie, the movie of my life! Running time: my whole life, my infinite existence. Producer: the Universe. Starring: Eva. Supporting roles: my friends from babysitting, the older people I've taken care of and all those that will come along. Secondary actors: some of my neighbors, those in the group, the doorman and everyone else that shows up that wants to take part.

Screenwriter: Eva. Director: Eva. Music, trills, humming and cackles: Eva.

Oof, it's time to get my butt off the chair. I can't fall asleep. I'm not going to have time to get bored. I've got to push a lot of buttons so that the film will be a critical and commercial success. From now on, I'm going to dedicate the time I usually waste on things that don't concern me on making some progress in shooting my great project: My Life.

I'm not organized, life overwhelms me. Time and money flee from me, and sometimes, loneliness appears, hand-in-hand with sadness and tears that leave me without the will to do anything, exhausted, stripped of my usual sense of humor. I hope that having left the group will change the scenery.

I am full of good intentions to clean and organize the apartment, to get rid of the mountains of prehistoric papers, and things that I don't need. However, in the fight against my exhaustion and apathy, my good intentions come out losing. Ugh, there's so much dust. I could make notes with my finger if I wanted. Housekeeping chores don't inspire me at all.

Rolling up my sleeves, washing the dishes, mopping and dusting are things that I'm awful at. "Home sweet home" is getting on top of me.

The call of the wild is my thing, the movement of the urban jungle. I'm charmed by the symphony of alarms, honking horns, bustling bars, stores, restaurants… Going from here to there, mingling with the diverse urban characters. Spinning like a carousel, absent-minded, disorients my sadness and my soul's nostalgia. It keeps my tears away, distracting them. I also know that it's drawing me away from myself, from my Inner Wisdom.

Wandering around the city, being outside, taking turn after turn, gives me the feeling that I'm getting closer to what I'm looking for, but in reality I have no idea what that might be…

I'm allergic to my apartment's walls. Maybe it's due to a subconscious fear that I have in finding myself, my historical ghosts. It's a problem I've got to solve now. I know that the silence, the quietness that I get in my home's peaceful oasis, can fill me with serenity and strength and can bring magic to my life.

I'm going to give myself the luxury of choosing that beautiful program. What was it called? The Whisperer… The Singer of Truth… The Sower of Truth? Let's see if I can remember what station it was… Ah ha, I marked it on the receiver with a little line… here It is, and it's on now. What luck! I found it, it's starting now:

"Hello friends, I love you. I'm the truth singer, as always with my heart ready to synchronize with yours.

You ask yourselves: Why does the singer generally address women? It's simple, more women than men watch my live show. Similarly with the radio audience. They're doing it for themselves.

This program is for all those who want to listen to it, of course. We don't marginalize anyone here. The show is for everyone, whether you live in a palace or sleep on cardboard. For the attractive or unattractive people. For those who listen in from other dimensions because they like our crystalline accent. For you, the feminine energy that you're emitting demonstrates that you're alive, vibrant, full of force and enthusiasm. For all those who desire to keep moving up, and for all those who desire to grow, it is up to you to advance faster. It depends on your desire to caress the stars.

And without further ado, today's light pearls travel from my heart to yours.

Look, an old apron can be more amazing than a luxurious evening gown. A shell found on the shore can be more amazing than any expensive necklace acquired at a jeweler's. Fresh bread from your grandmother's oven can be more amazing than dinner at the best restaurant. And that's how it works because this amazement is activated by emotion and deep feelings… And finally, what can be more amazing than a friendly voice, the glimmer of a tear of gratitude, an understanding look, an "I'm thinking of you", a "you're in my heart", an "I love you"…?

Do you see that homeless man? He's worth as much as you are. He's received the same quantity of Light from the Universe as you have. A smug smile appears on your face. Look up at the stars, if you can, if your neck isn't paralyzed from looking at the tips of your expensive trendy shoes and the stock market's fluctuating reports. What do you see? The sky. What else? The stars. And then if you keep looking, further and deeper with your heart, you'll see galaxies, millions of them, all of them with a myriad of stars. And if you keep looking, you'll get lost… because that infinity is a lot of infinity…

Your level of arrogance and importance has decreased. You're more on the homeless man's level, right? Look at him again. He's on his bench, contemplating the sky, ecstatic, surprised, captivated, seduced… Look closely at his eyes. They're smiling, sparkling with astonishment at such a vast grandness. He's mumbling something, very quietly: "Thank You for not having to pay You to see the stars… Thank You for listening to me when I open up my heart to You… Thank You for helping me at any moment and any place… Thank You for drying my tears… Thank You for not needing intermediaries to speak with You… Thank You for keeping me company, inside and outside… I love You…"

Look, one of the best things you can do for others is to let them live their own lives. Be sure to stay out of their flying space and that your wings don't touch theirs, disturbing their flight.

Before loving others you need to love yourself. It'll be difficult to love them, if you don't love yourself.

You don't believe in miracles? Take a good look at yourself. You're a great miracle! A miracle formed by the millions of intelligent and hard-working cells that form your body, that wonderful dwelling that houses your marvelous spirit, giving it the opportunity to express itself and to grow in matter, flying, laughing, crying, feeling, getting excited, loving…

I'm going to speak to you about Love, and I don't mean the tiny love, written in lowercase letters of selfishness, judgments and attachments. I'll speak to you of Love written with twinkling stars, of the Love written with your heart, with your emotions, with the Love Energy Spark that you carry inside of you.

When you welcome your Big Love, you will be filled with happiness and you will celebrate everything, even the tiniest details. You will be more tolerant of yourself, not condemning yourself like you used to. You will appreciate, value, applaud and give yourself pats on the back. You will recognize that you're a precious being.

Love thinks, says and does without announcing itself, silently, without making a scene. Love doesn't exhibit itself. It doesn't need to advertise itself. Why would it need to? It's there, like always, within anyone's reach.

When you embrace Love, your life will change. What's pointless, obsolete, will detach itself from you. It will be left behind and your sparkles will take their place.

What's your total success? To fill your life with love. To be Love and to love. You can give all that you want and you'll never run out. It's immediately replaced by the Universe.

When you're filled with Love and radiate it, everything changes around you, the magic of life chooses you as a partner and dances with you.

Your heart's love never abandons you, it always loves you. It diminishes your fears, protects, harmonizes, pacifies...

Love is inside and outside of you. Dedicate time to listen to what its silent words are saying to you.

In you, in everyone, Love Energy lives. It maintains the flame of your breath, life after life, in the fascinating voyage that allows you To Be, that takes you closer to the Creator.

Radiate your love and peace toward the people and places on Earth that need them. World peace depends on your heart's peace and love, and in all of its inhabitants.

Do you want to change your defects into qualities? So, fill them with Love and Light.

It's very likely that the desires that you intensify with your Love Energy will become a reality.

If you put more Love in your life, more Light, it will be easier to live.

When you get closer to Love, judgments go away, tolerance and understanding draw near.

The expansion of your consciousness has a price. You'll be able to pay for it with reflection, contemplation, meditation, patience, effort, strength, Love coins…

My suggestions are like little stars of light. You can choose the ones you want. You can also, if you want, connect them with a thread of light and make a necklace out of them. It's about having them present, not forgetting them, because they'll help you smile and be happy.

Until tomorrow, my friends. Thank you for your attention. Light, love and peace."

"To you, Singer of Truths, your words illuminate my path, they resonate in my heart like bells, waking it up. Thank you for your necklace. I'm wearing it right now. It's my secret, because it's invisible."

Let me see if I have any messages.

"Hey, sad lady. I have a new boyfriend, I'll introduce him to everyone at a dinner party in the club, we'll split the costs. Oh, remember, wear something elegant, don't wear your tears necklace. Call me for the details."

My tears necklace… Nice touch.

"Hi, honey. I'm almost finished with the sweaters, they're beautiful. The shops will be ripping them out of your hands. I've run out of balls of yarn. Can you loan me some money to buy some more? I'll pay you back with the sales commissions. Hope to hear from you soon. Hugs."

Like attracts like. Poverty attracts poverty.

"Hey, pathetic mermaid, Neptune talking..." Please, not the group's boring, dull, and tedious member. You're an interminable bore. I'm sick and tired of listening to your annoying stories again and again until I can't take it anymore. Your main topic is always "me, me, my, my." Your blah-blah-blah monotone is just the thing for insomnia. Record it onto a CD and you'll sell a ton. Listening to you makes me yawn uncontrollably. I fear your endless, overwhelming verbal serenades. I'll listen to you as background music, while I do other things...

Neptune's finished, it's been a short one...

Looks like there's another message. It sounds really far away and keeps breaking up... There's a lot of interference. I can only make out a few syllables. I'll try to listen to it again: "ppp... iii... eeess". I don't understand. They sound so far away, like a whisper. I'll listen again... Here they come, I'll concentrate all of my attention: "m... piii... eess." I'm trembling! It must have reminded me of something on a subconscious level. It's filled me with nostalgia.

I'll listen to it one more time. Full attention. I close my eyes to improve my concentration, I'll try to link the syllables: "mypincess" My princess! It's grandma! I've got goose bumps. It's her! I know it's her! I can feel it in the bottom of my soul. She's called me that so many times. The memories bring tears to my eyes. I know it's her! I've got a strong inner certainty. She's trying to contact me! She's tried to leave me a message through the phone. What could she be trying to tell me?

Grandma, I know that you can see me and hear my words as well as my thoughts. I have an idea, Grandma: get in touch with me, talk to me in my dreams, even though I'd prefer a telepathic dialogue, without having to be asleep. Maybe the dimensional receptiveness that I had when I was a child is a bit rusty for lack of use and it might not be possible.

I miss you Grandma. You were the only one who really loved me. You listened to me and understood me. You gave me advice and you comforted my sorrows. Why did you leave? I was left so alone, so forlorn. I noticed your absence so much, I still haven't gotten over it. I have such great memories of you, unforgettable ones. One day you told me: "Darling Evi, wherever you are and whatever you do, I'll always love you." It resounded so profoundly that I hugged you, weeping tears of inner joy.

A short time before you left, you told me, smiling: "Evi, remember that my spirit will be with you whenever you need it. Don't doubt that we'll keep finding each other in the eternity of our existence. Don't let my leaving make you sad. What we call death, here on earth, is really an end that's a beginning, a dawn. When my spirit abandons my body, it'll continue living in other beautiful spaces..."

For some reason, I've always refused to believe in life after death. I've stubbornly avoided the topic. I haven't been interested in seeing the documented evidence. I've rejected all of the books on it and testimonies that people have given about their experiences, their contact with family, friends or entities, from that place where we go after our transition.

This closed and negative attitude, which denied me the opportunity to reflect on the topic, has been something that hasn't done me any good. It makes me feel hopeless, afraid of death, and gives me a fragmented view of life which makes me distance myself from having a clear vision of what's essential for my personal growth. My grandma's phone call has awoken my belief in life after death.

My dislike toward paranormal topics comes from when I was a child. Strange things used to happen to me. I would see lights around people and, in my dreams, I would have premonitions. I could hear voices. I dreaded and feared some of the sensations that came along with those phenomenons. I wanted them out of my life. I closed the door and forgot them. From that point on, I began to free myself, avoiding conversations, books and everything that had to do with all of those topics.

From now on I'll think about the issue from an objective, neutral point of view. I'll leave behind my obstinate belief that life after death isn't real, especially when my heart is telling me "yes", that my grandma is still alive in another dimension, helping me.

An Ad Underlined in Blue

In this restaurant the early bird special breakfast price is exactly the money that I have left. I'm drawn to the pastry tray. It smells so good! I'm starving.

"Hey, honey, what are you going to have, the early bird special?"

Wow, what a friendly guy, I like his vibrations.

"Yes, I'll have that well done pastry over there."

"I'll give you this one, it's bigger, and it's also well done."

He's read my mind. What a nice smile! It's so warm and special.

"Here you go, beautiful, I hope you like it."

His eyes were fixed on me. He was staring at me with a goofy look and a satisfied smile on his face.

"Is something wrong?"

"You know what, you're pretty easy on the eyes."

"Thanks, you too. Is apple juice included?"

"Of course. Good choice. I can tell you know how to take care of yourself."

Easy on the eyes. Nobody had ever said that to me before. He's touched my heart… Mmmm, this pastry is yummy! It's good enough to lick my lips. I'm done with eating air sandwiches…

"Do you like the pastry?"

"It has an exquisite taste."

"Thanks, I made them. Here you go!"

"What's this? Another pastry!"

"It's a prize for giving your opinion. I saw how you closed your eyes with pleasure when you were savoring it. It was like an ovation to me. I had never seen anyone savor one of my pieces with such delight and concentration."

"They deserve it, they're the best."

"I'll leave you alone so that you can continue to savor it. This one has a bit of sesame."

"Eva, Eva!"

It's Ani, I hadn't seen her. She's calling me from the table at the back.

"Hi, Ani!"

"Eva, I'm so happy to see you. It's been almost a year."

"Yes, since the night we went out dancing with the group. You know what? I'm no longer with them."

"It was time to go. It was a relationship that no one could stand. You're going through a period of changes. They don't worry about changing their old habits. They're comfortable with them. They don't want to open themselves up to new things. They don't change, and they don't let others change. They dislike seeing people advance. How are your depression phases going? Have you gotten over them?"

"They're still there. They come and go. Sometimes I get very down, I just can't shake it off."

"You're an old spirit, Eva. Maybe, like I told you before, your sadness comes from a problem that you've dragged along from a past life. Maybe something or someone hurt you, traumatized you. When you identify the origin of your pain, your anguish will disappear and you'll heal emotionally. I suppose that you'll remember when your heart has enough comprehension and peace to forgive the cause of your sorrows.

Remember to ask for help. When you ask, you receive from Life. Before asking make sure that you know what you really want. Define your plea. Request with clarity and accuracy. Ask fervently, from the heart. Plead with certainty. The Universe is listening to your request and it will grant it but if you have doubt, or if you don't stand behind it with faith, it loses strength.

Your request might take time in arriving. It might wait until you're ready, until the right moment for your evolution. Take into consideration that Life is always on your side, even though sometimes it may appear as though it's not."

"Thanks, Ani, I'll take it into consideration. This morning I was listening to the phone messages and in the last one I was able to make out two words amid all of the noise: 'My princess'. I immediately remembered that my grandma used to call me that and I felt in my heart that it was her who was trying to send me a message. What do you think?"

"Yes, it's possible that it was your grandma. Maybe she has something to say to you or she's trying to help you remember where your trauma stems from, so then you would be able to free yourself from your sadness. Pay attention to your dreams and what you receive in your meditations, in your thoughts. Maybe she'll help you telepathically. It might be that she's trying to lower her vibration so that it will be closer to yours and facilitate the connection. As for you, put an effort into increasing yours."

"How do I increase it?"

"A healthy lifestyle, exercise, air, sun but with moderation. Eat foods that won't weigh your body down, reduce the amount of alcohol, tobacco, meat, fish that you consume. Eat more fruit and vegetables, drink mineral water with a low amount of dry residue. Try to drink and cook with mineral water instead of using tap water, your body will be thankful for that.

Practice meditating. It will help you to achieve mental tranquility.

Try to have pure, transparent and useful thoughts. Avoid wasting your energy on verbal arguments, trying to convince people of things that they don't want to be convinced of.

Practice yoga, walk. The movement will balance your energy points. Listen or sing mantras. Say positive affirmations. During the day keep your mind close to your heart's Love Energy.

"It's difficult, there are so many keys to touch."

"Yes, it is. It's not easy to change your habits and thoughts, but if you try to do it with strength and you maintain it, little by little you'll achieve it. Sorry, I have to go. I'm going straight to the airport, I don't want to miss my flight. I'll call you when I get back and we'll meet up when we both have the time."

"I hope so, Ani, give me a hug… Have a good flight."

"Thank you, keep in mind what we've talked about."

"Will do, Ani, take care."

Okay, I'll follow Ani's advice, I'll ask… from my heart, fervently: Creator, I beg that You free me from my tears and sadness, I've carried them for a long time. I also ask that You provide me with something so that I may come out of these hard financial times. Thank You.

Since I came in, I have been noticing the newspaper that's on top of that chair. Someone must have forgotten it. I'm going to take a glance at it.

It's open at the wanted ads… There's one underlined in blue… They want a translator, for a book… I could do that. What a coincidence! Could it be the answer to my request? It's five minutes from here. If I leave now and hurry, I might get there on time. I'll be the last in line, but it's worth a try… I'll say goodbye to the sweet pastry baker.

"See you later, pastry master. Thanks for your works of art."

"Thank you for coming. Don't forget to come back. Our energies connected."

"I'll anxiously wait to try another of your delicacies again."

"I hope that you come back to see the pastry maker, too."

"Of course, you're first on my priority list."

He's not that attractive, but his inner light attracts me. He would make such a great boyfriend. It's hard for me to leave…

I walk faster so that I can make it on time. It's near… ahh! I slipped. I almost fell. I stepped on dog shit. What bad luck! I've twisted my ankle. It hurts a lot. I hope I haven't dislocated it. I'll clean my shoe on the ground beside the tree. I clean it well to get rid of the smell…

I'm exhausted. The last thing I need now is to start limping. I can see stars when I lean on my foot. It's sad that there are people who are so inconsiderate to others. I'm on the verge of crying. I can't go to the interview now. What a pitiful image I must be! Where am I going looking so graceless? Straight to failure, to the obvious answer: "The position has been filled." I'm going to leave. No! I'm going to stay. Perhaps this is the Universe's answer to my request.

They're not looking for a convention translator or interpreter. Book translation can be done at home, with bad hair, in curlers and slippers. What's important is the quality of the work, not personal presentation. I'll wait until the end. There's the hotel. I take three deep breaths. Here I go, standing tall and limping, but with a confident walk. I'll ask at reception.

"Mr. Ricard, please."

"Yes, he's that gentleman at the back, the one that's with the young lady. You can wait in the lobby."

"Thank you."

Where's the line? There are only two people! The blonde he's talking to and me. She's like a model. All cleavage, in an elastic mini skirt, wearing a blouse a size too small, TV make-up and she's using her curves generously. She's playing her winning cards, and she has the advantage. She's already counting the money. She's working him really well. She's going to walk away with the job. She's a professional. She's using all of her seduction weapons on him. She's going to have cramps in her lips for smiling so much. She smiles even with her ears. She's not threatened by me and she figures she's got the job in the bag.

He's entertained, looking at her as if she were the musical hit of the season. I look horrible. He might be shocked when he sees me. I smell like sweat, and maybe there's still a trace of that dog shit on me. Jeans torn over time and lack of money. Bags under my eyes from not having slept last night. I'm limping. I look like a scarecrow.

He's so fascinated by the girl that he probably hasn't noticed that there's another candidate waiting. They're having a great time. They are laughing together. I feel awful. My morale is low. Every interview is a nightmare. Sometimes, I even get a rash. I'm very sensitive to rejection. It takes me a long time to get over it.

He only has eyes for her. Three's a crowd. I have no chance. Nil. I'm going to leave. This is an escape! I won't throw in the towel. I'll continue until the end. I won't give up! I close my eyes, breathe deeply, calmly, again, no hurry, peacefully. I'm alive. I'm going to enjoy the moment, the situation, and the setting's colors to the fullest, regardless of the interview's result. I'll take it as a learning experience.

"Eva, please."

It's him! He's calling me. He's said goodbye to her! She walks away with an unfriendly face. Where did you lose your smile?

He's really tall. He has such a nice smile. How does he know my name? I didn't give it to the receptionist. He's addressed me like we know each other, no "Miss." He's got a really deep look. He's thin. He's not that young. He's wearing a pale suit made out of linen, moccasins, collarless shirt, long hair…

We walk towards each other. He is smiling warmly with his right arm and hand slightly open in a welcoming way. It looks like he's moving in slow motion. I feel like I'm floating, weightless. He shakes my hand. It's hard to describe the peaceful sensation that I have in his presence. He silently looks at me, as if he's known me forever, with the joy that an anticipated encounter produces. Time passes by slowly, I'm wrapped by familiar, timeless sensations. It's an instant that tastes like eternity. Time loses strength. It fades. I don't remember why I'm here. His hand transmits protection. He finishes his long and warm handshake. Back to the present. I'm here for the book translation ad.

"Hello, Mr. Ricard, a pleasure to meet you."

"Hi, Eva. What do you say if we drop the "mister" and speak informally?"

"Fantastic. I feel more comfortable with it, too."

"My friends call me Ric."

"I like it. It's short and it sounds good."

"Shall we sit?"

His words have just brought me back to reality. What a comfortable armchair. I feel so relaxed. A soft euphoria comes over me. He's such a peaceful person. He doesn't seem to be in any kind of hurry. He's savoring the moment. He seems just as comfortable with me as I am with him. I feel so relaxed. He radiates great human warmth. He could be from anywhere. He doesn't have an accent and he expresses himself correctly.

"Do you like butterflies, Eva?"

"Yes, ever since I was little. Their agility, their beautiful colors... I have always been fascinated by their spins and turns. My grandmother, before putting me to bed, at the beginning of the protection prayer would say: Put your hands together, Evi, like a butterfly when it folds its wings, which makes it look as if it's praying."

"Great, you'll find the translation easier because it is about butterflies."

He's saying it as if I already had the job!

"Here's the manuscript. There are, approximately, half a million characters. About three-hundred pages. The job's yours, Eva."

Great! Great! Great!

"Is it all right if I give you an advance and pay you the rest when you've finished translating?"

"Yes, it's not a problem. How much time do I have to do the translation?"

"How about six months? The first of June at nine o'clock. Is that okay?"

"Perfect. I won't have to write down the date in my agenda because it's my birthday." He's writing out a check! I'm seeing it, but I can't believe it.

"Here you go. I've made it out to cash. That way you can cash it at the bank that's on your way out, on the corner just to the right."

Wow! It's a ton of money and it's only an advance. And here I was thinking I was a loser.

"If you think it's not enough, it can be increased."

"It's fine Ric. Thank you."

"I'm happy you've agreed to do the job, Eva."

"And I'm glad you've trusted me to do it, Ric."

"Eva, you've opened the door so that magic can enter your life."

"How have I done that?"

"You've given a big and strong "yes" to changes, truth, being faithful to yourself, to your inner strength, and to expanding your consciousness."

"You're saying such nice things, Ric."

"It's not difficult. I'm reading them in you, Eva. They must be about to close the bank. If you hurry, you'll be able to cash it."

"Yes, that's a good idea. I almost forgot. I better take off. See you on the first of June."

"I'll be here. We'll celebrate your birthday."

"It'll be one of my best birthdays ever."

"Yes it will, Eva. Good luck."

"Thank you, Ric. You, too."

I'm floating. The pain in my ankle has gone. What a strange interview! What a special person, so pleasant! A very beautiful energy was floating around us. It's been a magical morning... Thank You, Creator, for listening to me, for answering my plea, for having filled the hand I put out to You. Thank You for your messengers: Ric and the platinum blond, her underline in the newspaper and Ric's book were your answers to my request.

I'm lucky this bank is from the same chain where I have my account... He's verifying the signature on the check. The worst case scenario is that Ric put the wrong date, or the signature is a little different and doesn't match the one on file, or maybe he forgot to dot the *i*. Will the check bounce? I've got to stop thinking negatively! I'm going to think about good things and good things will happen. I'll get the money, I'm sure about that.

He looks up at me and stares, not saying anything. Why doesn't he speak? This is so suspenseful. It's taking an eternity. Does he think that I found the check, or is he hypnotized by my beautiful eyes?

"Would you like to deposit or cash the check?"

What a relief! It's music to my ears.

"I'll take two-hundred in cash, deposit the rest."

This is great, I'll be able to pay my late utility bills and the monthly costs for my sponsored child.

I'll have running water! I'll be able to shower without a jug of water. Goodbye fountain at the corner. I'm going to start working on the translation of the butterfly manuscript.

I'm going to start practicing meditation. I'm going to set-up a home oasis. I'm going to learn to like being with myself without needing others. It'll be my desert retreat. My truce with urban chaos.

I'd almost forgotten, how did Ric know my name? I just don't understand this translation thing, it's like something out of a novel. There are things that don't make sense: How can he pay me so much in advance without knowing me? Why didn't he ask for a receipt? Why didn't he ask me for ID? Not even my phone number. And, he said "see you in six months!" instead of the day after tomorrow. My rational, mistrusting and fearful mind is murmuring reasons why I shouldn't trust Ric, but my heart tells me that Ric is honest. My heart never lies. It's my brain that's always confusing me.

What about the underlined ad in the newspaper? No one knew that I was going into that coffee shop. I randomly went in there. When I walked in I saw the newspaper there, left behind on a chair…

An Oasis in the City

Translating the book is forcing me to be isolated at home and it's hard. I'm determined to feel comfortable in the apartment. We'll see… I've survived the first part of it. Solitude is shaking me up a lot. I'm able to stand the translation by altering it with other activities that distract and motivate me: going down to the little garden, looking at people, watching children play, walking on earth and filling up on the trees' energy is good for me. It takes away the stress of being locked up in the apartment, burning my eyes with the translation. I meditate and do yoga, they quiet my mind and ease my loneliness. When I'm feeling down, I listen to music or dance, making my energy move and stopping me from feeling sad. I practice breathing and saying positive affirmations. They calm me. I read an interesting book or go for a walk. I don't cultivate my loneliness or feel sorry for myself… It's about substituting my sorrows for something else.

It was a good idea to use my translating time also as a semi-meditation practice. Before starting to write, I sit down with a straight back, so that the cosmic energies can flow better through my light channel. My arms comfortably relaxed. I take a few conscious breaths and focus my attention on the translation, making sure I don't let any unrelated ideas invade my mind.

I also take advantage of this time to get used to behave calmly, enjoying the work, the moment. I allow myself to stop and enjoy the luxury of feeling my breathing from time to time. Before, I never took breaks. I lived each day as if it were a continuous obstacle race. Now, I try to live it like a pleasant walk, and I stop from time to time to enjoy the small things I see on the way. I'm making my life simpler and easier. I don't waste my precious time on activities, issues and people that aren't good for me. I have fortified my "No, thank you" for invitations or things I don't feel like doing, without giving lengthy explanations. I say something brief: "My schedule is over packed" and I'm set on my decision, unless there are changes in my plans. Making excuses is a thing of the past. In general, I don't stay out late. I go to bed early and I get up early. Being without a TV gives me more free time. I've started to read grandma's books.

I've finally started to practice meditation. Everything has its right moment. I used to have the wrong idea about what meditation was. I thought it was about focusing one's attention on a topic, an idea, a plot, and reflecting upon it, thinking about it over and over.

Now I know that meditation is about trying to relax my mind, emptying it of thoughts, giving them a vacation. Focusing all of my attention on keeping my mind's space clear, quiet, freeing it of ideas. To achieve this, I focus and fix all of my attention on my breathing or on repeating a positive affirmation or mantra, making sure that my concentration doesn't lose strength and that it becomes like a swirling leaf blown by the wind. During meditation, I set my mind to "silent emptiness" instead of "half-full", "stocked-full", or "overflowing".

Okay, I'm going to meditate for awhile. Let's see how it goes. I get comfortable, so that a bad posture won't hinder my concentration. My knees hurt today, so I'll sit on a chair or in an armchair, instead of with my legs crossed on my cotton pillow. My clothes and belt shouldn't be tight. Nothing should bother me. Straight back, so that energy can easily run through my spine, my light channel. I close my eyes, relax my body and remove tension from my muscles.

I put all of my thoughts, plans, worries and fears to one side. I focus all of my attention on breathing or the repetition of a positive affirmation, so that it doesn't move from here to there because of my impulsive thoughts. It's how I close thoughts off from my mind so that they can't enter, so that they find the space occupied, full of a strong silence.

I go down and install my mind in my heart's calm, quietness, empty of thoughts, silent. Inside, only silence, forging peace, fullness. If a thought comes near, I don't fight it, I just let it pass by, I avoid the challenge, the tournament, bringing back my attention to the great pleasure of breathing. Once again, my mind is like a clear sky without a single cloud. I notice how peace grows within me. It's such a pleasant state, it makes me want to continue with the exercise, the absence of thoughts, the receptive silence...

I can maintain a certain meditative state during the day, focussing my attention on what I'm doing, by making sure that no stray thoughts enter my mind, distracting it from its tasks. I can't reach the same deep state as if I were only meditating, where all of my attention is focused on emptying my mind, freeing it, making it available, but it's good to keep it active, making it stronger... Some tasks get me closer to this meditative state than others. They're the ones that need more attention: studying, painting, writing, listening to music...

Being inside my home oasis, far from the teeming bustle of the streets and the non-stop unnecessary obligations, continues to be difficult, but every day less so. It's giving me a serenity and an inner peace that I didn't have before. Freeing my schedule of social activities that didn't appeal to me, and going less to the movies, to dinner, shopping with people or alone... has left me with more free time to do the essential things: passing all of my remaining classes, increasing my state of consciousness, meditating, discovering what a beautiful being I am, putting my changes into effect and, of course, enjoying my free time doing my favorite things and allowing myself to be fascinated by the wonder of life.

I plan my activities, allowing myself to change plans when I feel something unexpected is coming, a situation, an impulse, a feeling... No inflexible, immobile, rigid positions.

I don't need to change places so much in search of emotions. I can also find amusement and adventure in my own inner melodies. This is a reflection phase that I've been waiting for and needed. I've started it well and I'm putting a lot of effort into maintaining it.

I get up, stiff from sitting for such a long time. I'll mop the floor to get my body moving. I should mop my mind too. It's busy thinking over the same nonsense that my paper palace is made out of. It leaves me without time to go out to the garden of the present and bathe in its fragrances. Only a few drops fall from my life's faucet. I have to make a decision to open it all the way so that it flows invigoratingly. If my ego spends the entire day dressing up in front of the mirror, it will make my world very tiny, miserly and grey. I'll lose life's wonders, they'll pass me by and I won't even notice.

However, I'm making progress. My stages of peace, serenity and mental quietness are more and more frequent. I think they must be coming from my grandma's books, my meditations and the translation work. They quiet my mind and take me away from the annoying racket of public places.

The splendid dreams I've had about grandma comfort me a lot. I'm so lucky to be able to remember her messages when I wake up. I love some of them, they're suitable for framing: "Eva, you're entering a phase where you'll receive many gifts. Be alert. Have a quiet mind so that you won't miss any of them. Be yourself. Be true to what your heart tells you, it's your great master."

I've found something that keeps me entertained 24 hours a day. The biggest show in the world: Myself! I've got the best front row seat and a lifetime free pass. The stage is full of actors that interact with me. I can change the script any time I want. It's open to constant revisions. I allow myself, the actors and Life to improvise. It's more amusing this way, more creative. I can't stop surprising myself with the deployment of all my resources, my creativity and interpretive knowledge.

I don't want my mood to depend upon the company of others, on their flattery, their applauses, on the attention that they give me. I want to feel okay even when I'm alone, without needing an entourage of fools praising and flattering my little ego. I want to fill myself with fulfilment, happiness and love. I'm going to make a plan to achieve this, but first I have to overcome my sorrow. It's what pushes me toward others in search of consolation and what takes away my will to live. At the moment they're in the script, but I've got a feeling that their role is about to end.

I'm opening myself up to inspiration, creativity, changes, to new things. I've stopped looking at my bellybutton and I've opened myself up to diversity, to life's adventure which surrounds me. I'm balancing the "me" with the "you", "us", "them"... with the Universe.

I'll leave some space in my schedule for unexpected, spontaneous things... for the tiny and light feather that settled on my arm this morning, sent by Life on a breeze. It brought a message: "Eva, stop hurrying, live each moment, exalt yourself with my beautiful colors, accentuated by the sunlight, gaze at me with wonder, admiration, respect and humility because the Universe is in me."

Before, when Life handed me its glass of nectar, I passed by it quickly, without stopping my race, almost knocking the tray over and I said, panting: "Some other time. I don't have a second to spare," without even thanking it for its gesture that it won't offer me again. I've lost many of its gifts because of my hurry. I'll learn how to stroll and when I see it coming I'll stop and hold out my cup to receive the gift it offers me. I'll show my gratitude and, in its company, I'll savor its ambrosia with all of my senses.

I'm going to take a shower. I visualize a rain of infinite sparks of light from the Universe falling over me, cleaning, purifying my body and energy layers around it. Also I think it takes away some of my body's static electricity...

I'm lucky that I've got this little garden next to my house. These trees must be a hundred years old. The people planning the underground parking garage in the square suggested removing the trees and replanting them once the project was finished. The idea was so stupid, I don't even think they thought it was a good one. The neighborhood mobilized against pulling out the majestic trees. They stuck together and won. We were able to save the green space. Another small lung for a city that is covered by so much asphalt and cement that it can hardly breathe. I can tell that walking on Mother Earth and filling myself with the trees' energy revitalizes me. It's enchanting to see how the birds and clouds chase each other. Children entertain themselves with such ease. They can create toys out of anything, forgetting everything that isn't part of the fun. They've woken up the disheartened little girl that's inside of me.

Again, I foresee the winds of sadness announcing tears. I don't feel like doing anything, not even continuing the translation. I'm on schedule and I can take a day off. I haven't listened to the singer of truths in days. She cheers me up... This is her radio station:

"Hello, friends. I'm back with my basket of truths that will put you in the eye of your confusion's hurricane.

Sometimes my whispering voice will sound like a lullaby. In other moments, it will sound harsh and loud, to wake up those people who are sleeping in the back rows.

Don't sign-up for a marathon and make your body finish with a good time. Instead, run at a leisurely pace, alone or with friends, without competing to see who runs faster or better. Run for the pleasure of feeling your body move, to share the race together, to feel the breeze and to enjoy the landscape. Stop, once in awhile, so that your eyes can take in the surroundings.

Open your eyes, open your ears, open your words, open your hands, open your smile, open your mind, open your heart, open your love, activate yourself. You're alive!

Unwrap your sense of humor, try out your smile and your laugh again, awaken your curiosity and get out of your comfort zone. Send your little ego on vacation…

Life hands you the perfect script. It provides the actors, the stage and your breath. You read it and start making changes, crossing things out, scribbling over everything. Later, you don't like how it turned out. You've made a mess and you don't know how to unravel the ball of yarn. You get tired and you blame Life, telling it that its script is mediocre, and you forget about it.

Do you know what takes the fun out of your life? You want everyone to applaud you. You're paying attention to whether they'll cheer or jeer you. It's a pity. You miss the best of life: playing for fun, to distract you and to laugh. Concentrate on the game, feel its emotion, play with it and have a good time. Don't worry if they're filming you.

Don't believe that to be fascinated you have to go around the world. Fascination can be found in the smallest things that come to you over the course of a day, in your surroundings and in your inner landscapes.

I suggest you sign-up for a master's degree. Forget the price. Life gives it to you. You have the best master, without needing to go to some faraway mountaintop sanctuary, because your master, your Inner Master, is inside you. You only have to lower your mind, silently, to his core and listen to him. If you follow his teachings you'll end up being an expert in the art of living. You'll find the path to love, the Big Love… Ah, the degree is called: "I'm Love and I love" or if you prefer the shorter version: "I love," simple as that.

There are issues, enmities, knots left tied that you've dragged along with you from one incarnation to another. You didn't know how to untie them, which is why Life keeps presenting them to you with the same characters over and over again. You'll keep encountering each other so that you can settle the matter once and for all. Wrap everyone up who's involved in it, yourself included, with light, love, peace and forgiveness. Cut, once and for all, those rancid and unfinished stories that are hindering your evolution. You'll walk easier without all that baggage.

You spend your life dragging along a carriage full of things that you don't need, which robs you of your time and energy, and takes the glow out of your life. Decide to shake the excess weight off your back.

Remember that being in a good mood and being happy are tools that will be useful to simplify your life… and others'.

Don't always walk with a stopwatch in your hand. Take the time you need to feel life. Don't gobble it up, taste it.

If you go through life without judging, directing your attention to the brilliance of others instead of to their limitations, stars will rain over you and you'll see how many friends you'll find.

Appreciating the small details is what gets us closer to happiness and fulfillment. Remember that the immense sea is made out of humble drops.

It's not easy to live in a society as complicated as ours. To confront its difficulties you need to be balanced, in contemplation and action.

Before starting a project you need to consider whether it's really necessary and ask yourself if it comes from your heart, if it agrees with your inner feelings. That way, you'll avoid conflicts, you'll be more satisfied with yourself and you'll have more time and energy.

It's about time you overcame your arrogance and polished your humility, naturalness and strength.

When you go into your heart, your smile is reborn and your furrowed brow disappears.

You're growing. There are attitudes that can no longer touch you. The only person that can get rid of them is you. Give them a loud "no" so that they can hear it, stick a stamp on them and mark it urgent, but don't write the return address.

Head toward your ethereal white sled. Get in and take off. Using your radiant breath, fly toward your heart. Smoothly make contact. Descend and direct yourself to your balcony, the best place to feel the Universe. Get comfortable, quiet your mind, feel it… You're attracted to its sublime magnificence so much that you get close to its pulse, its frequency, its music. You're certain that every time that you lower your mind to your heart you'll have gotten a little closer to its greatness.

Before finishing, I want to earnestly ask you for a favor: don't put me up on a pedestal. I'm at the same level as you. We've all received the same amount of Light. The only difference is the dedication and enthusiasm that everyone puts into peeling off the layers that cover their inner diamond. We're all on the path and we'll all get there, some earlier and others later. The important thing is to get there. We'll all find each other in the Light. Until next week, my friends. From my heart, light, love and peace."

Singer of Truths, thank you again for your pearls of wisdom. They stimulate me, get me to the starting line.

I know I'm dreaming. I know the dream is real and it's happening in the space where I am. I'm in a place full of love and peace. I've been invited. It's an assembly, a meeting of sages. I don't know if I'll remember it when I wake up…

I've woken up. What a shame! It was so interesting. I found myself so comfortable in that place with the light beings. I'll try to fall asleep again so I can go back to the same dream… I'm dreaming again… I can't go back to the assembly of wise beings.

I'm in a valley, surrounded by mountains. On the highest point, I see a white horse with its rider. The steed leaps into the air, spreading its beautiful wings and flying. It's coming towards me! It's very quick, almost here. A woman is riding it! The horse stops in front of me. She looks at me and smiles. She dismounts with an agile jump, and stands in front of me. She joins the palms of her hands and puts them in front her heart. She greets me: "I bow reverently to you, I honor the Universe of love and peace that resides within you. In your core, you and I are one." I return the greeting: "I feel intensely lucky to meet you and know that you're in my heart." She's my inner warrior, she's me! She offers me a little

45

sack. I open it and light comes pouring out from inside. There are four sparkling quartz pyramids. It's a beautiful gift. I raise my eyes to thank her but she's gone, vanished, trailing a strong rose smell.

The translation is forcing me to stay in the apartment. It is a peaceful time that's helping me start some of the things that are on my to-do list:

Let's see... I took the car to the junk yard. I've rented out my parking space. I've resisted the draw of the group's tempting invitations and I haven't answered their insistent calls. I'm still taking care of my beloved kids and old folks. There are some that I don't even charge as there's no better payment than enjoying their company and kindness. They're precious, they know when I'm lonely and they encourage and cheer me up.

I feel comfortable without having people around me singing me praises. I'm learning how to appreciate, love, tolerate myself, to be my own best friend, instead of being the pigheaded enemy that I used to be, who judged and underestimated me. I no longer have to beg for friendship, I give it to myself, I lavish myself with it, without skimping.

I keep on making my life simpler. I'm getting rid of useless things that wasted my time and energy.

I'm mindful of myself during the day, aware of my thoughts, words and actions. This helps me to find and recognize myself, to become conscious of the qualities I have and the ones I lack.

I'm making a lot of progress in quieting my mind, focusing my attention. I've sent some thoughts that blinded me out to pasture. They no longer enter my mind.

This peacefulness makes a lot of my errors visible. I've wasted a lot of time, energy and self-esteem on pleasing others, instead of loving myself. This withdrawal is helping me break old habits that have hindered my advancement. I'm incorporating new habits into my life, more fulfilling ways to live.

I'm done with my last disorientated phase. A time when I didn't take good care of my body and soul, offering them unhealthy food and drinks, and spending time with people who held me back.

I go to bed early now. I used to go to bed at seven in the morning, and now I wake up at that time. What a change! Before, I would get up with a hangover and drag myself out of bed half-asleep. Now, I get up with my mind and body well rested and I start meditating and doing yoga exercises. It's a good thing that I had to sell the TV. It would have kept me on the sofa and I'd have gone to bed really late.

I dedicate a part of each day to recycling the pile of things that I don't need anymore: papers, junk, clothes… I only want to have a few belongings, keeping just the essential things that I need to take care of my body and soul.

The time I dedicate to quieting my mind increases my inner peace and helps my general advancement.

I'm freer, I don't dance to anyone else's song, I choose my own music, my own dance, my own songs.

Ani has given me some beautiful music with sublime voices that elevate my soul and transport me to the magical peace of my inner world.

In my shortsightedness, I chose activities that left me without any time to do the crucial things, like putting my longed for changes into effect. I threw out diamonds and spent my time collecting pebbles. That's history now. Now I thread more carefully.

I see the translation as a puzzle, like fitting colored words together until finishing the game, instead of as a job. I translate relaxed, calm, it helps me practice being still and appeased, which is something I need.

I'm very happy to be finally comfortable at home, feeling this gratified sensation of liking and loving myself. This is great, I'm learning how to be still, silent, without a muddled mind. I'm making progress.

I'm delighted that I've started to read grandma's books. They've been waiting for me for a long time. Thank you, grandma. You chose your books well and you made them your friends. You left your vibration in them, your intense desire for knowledge, your aspiration to discover truths, your wish to grow, your immense love for life. Your attitude lives on in my heart's music, dance and songs. Your teachings left a luminous mark on me that will always last. I love you, grandma.

I honestly and patiently accept that my old habits will take some time to go away, it's normal, they've been with me for centuries. I don't adopt strict, demanding, rigid positions with my way of being. I look at my good side, my lights, which I used to think I didn't have or were burnt out. I've stopped worrying if others accept or reject me. I don't give up, nor do I stop being true to myself in order to receive some crumbs of appreciation, affection, friendship, love, applauses… I don't overexert myself trying to prove that I'm worth something and that I'm appreciated. I don't think that I'm less than others. I know I'm a wonderful being. I no longer waste time and energy with that whole thing. I'm tired of ceding my power to others.

I don't rebel against my moments of distress and unknown sadness. I recognize, accept and take responsibility for them. I will deal with them, the best way that I can, until they go away. I think that everything that's in my life is good for my personal growth. I think it helps me fine tune my patience, sensibility, humility, strength, my humanity…

I'm achieving the unimaginable, feeling good at home with myself. The tasks that I used to hate, I now love. I deserve some praise: "Eva, a big applause for you, you're working so hard to put your changes into effect." Now I have a good resource for facing my great and urgent desire to be always flitting about the street: I put on some relaxing music, it calms me down. I straighten my back, close my eyes and start breathing through my nose, gently, lengthening my breaths a bit. Taking great pleasure in breathing allows me to silence my mind and enter my soul's serenity.

I'm going to take a break. I've made some progress on the translation and I'm sick of words. I'm going to practice smiling. It puts me in a good mood and makes me happy. It's a good trick to ward off my sorrows. I release my smile, keeping it on my lips and in my heart while I dance to this inspirational music. I smile and smile again… I don't get tired of smiling… My feet dance and so does the smile on my lips, reaching the farthest corner of my body, and all of my cells, filling them with euphoria. This is great, the smiles and the dancing have increased my endorphins, the happiness hormones.

Loo-Chi-Chi

I can feel a load of depressing thoughts coming. When they reach my mind they won't be able to get in. They'll find the space occupied by the story I'm going to make up to tell my inner child. It'll be a funny story, sprinkled with fine irony to bring her heart's smile back. It'll act like a firewall against those huge clouds that announce a storm of sorrows. I think it's a good idea. Smile in the face of adversity. I'll trade tears for smiles. A cheery note has the ability to relax a tense situation, to cheer-up low emotional states, and it'll convert my furrowed brow into a smile.

My desire is for it to bring wide smiles to my lips, but I'll be equally satisfied if only my heart and mind feel their soft touch. I dedicate this story to you, my dear inner child, so that you may dream... smiling. Let's see how my inspiration is doing.

I'll consciously draw in some calming breaths that will intensify my imagination. I'll close my eyes and identify myself with the characters, their circumstances, their ups and downs, their difficulties... I'll color them with my soul's emotions. Let's see what I can come up with...

I'll start the story at the beginning of humanity, when someone made fire for the first time.

A group of hominids live, very precariously, in an enormous cave near a river.

One of the boys runs around the jungle when suddenly he sees a girl, who must be about his age, next to a bush. They look at each other strangely and curiously. She is spread out on the ground, motionless. The boy pokes her with a branch. The girl neither moves nor shows fear. He helps her stand up and when he lets her go, she collapses. She can't stand up! He tries several times, but whenever he lets her go, she always falls. She doesn't have strength in her arms or legs. She can't walk.

The young primate moves away from her, stops, half turns around and stares at her for a long time. He goes back to her, puts her on his back and heads back to his tribe's cave.

The members of the group look at her with hostility. She has some physical differences to them: her forehead is wider, her big toes are straight, parallel to the others... "How does she hold onto branches?" Eventually, they get tired of looking at her and abandon her in a corner, forgetting her and leaving her to her own devices. She makes faces to call attention to herself, so that they'll bring her something to eat. No one pays attention to her. They completely ignore her.

She survives thanks to her little friend who feeds and protects her. If someone comes close to her with bad intentions, he bares his teeth and growls, throws rocks at them, and does everything possible to protect her. He puts her on his back and takes her everywhere he goes. He sits her down and surrounds her with branches so that she can sit up and won't fall over.

Her lips start curving upwards and maintain an expression of pure happiness, produced by the great delight she has in contemplating the magnificent show that life puts on for her at every moment. Sometimes she closes her eyes, keeping her lips curved. Could it be a smile?

The members of the group are amazed by watching her. No one in their group has ever made such a strange and fascinating gesture with their lips! They don't tire trying to imitate her strange grimaces.

They began to copy everything she did. They closed their eyes when they shouldn't, like when they ran. They bumped their heads often. They were pretty ignorant, but they had a strong desire to learn.

The girl lifted her hand slowly, with difficulty, due to her reduced mobility and, placing it on the boy's chest said, "Moo-ti-ti, Moo-ti-ti, Moo-ti-ti." Pointing to herself she repeated patiently, "Loo-chi-chi, Loo-chi-chi," until the boy understood and learned.

Moo-ti-ti ran wildly from one place to another, all day yelling to the whole tribe, "Moo-ti-ti, Moo-ti-ti, Moo-ti-ti," all the while hitting himself on his chest like a gorilla.

For several days, the settlement was like a cage of crickets, everyone desperately running around, hoarsely yelling strange guttural sounds and banging on their chests almost to the point of breaking them. And smiling! If they continue advancing at this rate, soon they'll be paying taxes…

Loo was a natural-born observer. She would spend hours and hours just contemplating, contemplating and contemplating. It was her favorite sport. This is the way she began to strengthen her mind and develop her brain's right hemisphere. She was like a tree, perceiving everything around her. She became a passive spectator. She was the prelude to the phenomenon that would appear ages later, the button-clicker primate, the television watcher, the compulsive consumer of images.

Only Loo could have done it, she began the transition from the Stone Age up to the age of the Remote Control Button.

She handled her inability to move in a good way and very calmly, without the smallest complaint. It was touching to see how lovingly her protective friend treated her. She wasn't very pretty, but her inner brightness shone from within and made her beautiful. To her friend, she was the most attractive girl in the world.

She discovered that she could mentally communicate with him. She had just opened language's faucet, that goes hand-in-hand with thinking and understanding. Was Loo-chi-chi the missing link between humans and chimps? Almost certainly.

Compared to them, Loo is a lynx. They need to get hit on the head with a coconut to know that they're standing under a coconut tree. She intuits the miracle, the invention from afar. It hits them in the face and they push it aside, without seeing it. Their level of consciousness needs to improve significantly to be on the same level as Loo. Where did you come from, Loo? From the stars, right?

She became a legend. Her prodigious mind initiated a ton of innovative advances that still exist today.

What motivates them is food, so when they kill a dinosaur, they go a long time without doing anything other than eating and sleeping, yawning and sleeping, burping loudly and sleeping… Heavy digestion leaves them lethargic, in a state of drowsiness, which limits their flow of ideas.

One day, Loo amusingly painted her face and body with white clay. When the tribe members saw her, they were petrified, amazed, with their mouths hanging open, astonished with admiration. It's wonderful! They instantly copied everything she did. They spent the whole day covering each other in mud like crazy, leaving the settlement oozing with sludge. She was the pioneer of the booming make-up industry. What a marvelous brain!

From then on, it was out of control. If she yawned, they yawned. If she scratched her eye, they scratched theirs. They didn't have anything else to do, most of the time they followed the boy in throngs, with Loo hanging off his back. They revered her.

They also carried her around on their shoulders on a sort of wooden chair that she invented. They gave her the best place next to the fire and the best pieces of meat and fruit. They adorned her with flowers. They would constantly entertain her. She let them please her and she accepted all of their good deeds.

The children entertained themselves throwing rocks from the high point of the settlement. The rocks rolled down the hill, bouncing, and when they reached the bottom, they struck each other and cracked, delighting the children. She latched onto the idea like an eagle to its prey. To make a flint, you only need to hit two rocks together!

One day, Loo, fascinated by the spectacle she was watching, was hit by a shard of rock which cut her leg. She reflected, reflected and reflected for a long time, and suddenly, the corners of her mouth started to curve... the light bulb over her head had lit up. She made her ideas reality by putting Moo-ti-ti to work.

There was Moo, in the middle of a bunch of branches, sticks, vines and flints, taking mental orders from Loo. Devotedly transforming his girlfriend's instructions into brand new prototypes. She made him tie a sharp flint to a stick and invented the lance and harpoon. She instructed Moo to cut the stick, from which she got three more tools: the axe, the hammer and the knife. These inventions, apparently simple, were the beginning of the leather industry. Loo was unstoppable. Amazing. A genius in the prehistoric age, singlehandedly inaugurating and launching the age of Homo abilis, the tool maker.

Drawing on her previous observations she decided to tie a flexible stick to a vine, so that when it was tightened, it would launch a thin stick with a sharp flint tied to one of its sides. She had just invented the bow and arrow. The tribe was amazed by it. They could now kill animals from afar. They would huddle around her, with curved lips and they would hit their fists together... The first applause in history!

Her fame spread like wildfire to the other settlements. They came from all over, fascinated by the new tools, making impatient, long lines to see them. They brought various items to trade for the innovative tools. The primate had definitively converted itself into a tool maker. In that exact moment, the compulsive consumer was born. Loo became legendary. However, time erased all trace of her.

That rejected girl had become the brightest star in a group of copycats. They venerated and admired her so much that they followed her everywhere.

All right, one must admit that they were a little crude, but they weren't dumb and they were very appreciative. They knew how to value the comfort and security that Loo's creative genius was providing them. Her prestige rose so fast that they made her the head of the tribe.

Loo created the first matriarchal community. Lots of things changed: organized labor, no more disorder, equal opportunities, more refined manners, balancing the rational and the intuitive…

Thanks to Loo, history took a big leap forward.

From Loo's palace of trunks and branches, Moo emerges, pulling a kind of sled with Loo seated inside it, looking happy and satisfied.

Closely behind follow one, two, three, now four, five, six, seven children jumping and fighting in the midst of all the commotion. They all have their mom's birthmark: Loo's wide forehead and smile…

My inner child hadn't had such a good time in a long time. I've been identifying myself with the characters. Humor and irony haven't stopped me from asking myself some questions about Loo and Moo's adventures. I'll think about them at another time and see what conclusions I arrive at. The story has allowed me to escape my sorrows and cheer me up. Mission accomplished.

My Prodigious Changes

Thanks to my emotional stability and the free time I now have, I've begun the stage I was looking forward to: dusting off the changes that were waiting to be put into action. I've brought them together, a little disorganized, into one list entitled: *My Prodigious Changes.*

I write them down in the present instead of the future tense, thus making them more effective. Instead of *I'll smile more,* I write *I smile more.* Instead of *I'll exercise more,* I write *I exercise more.*

No unnecessary running around. Goodbye, speed. No more thinking, doing and speaking as if every minute might be my last. I'm going to stop my unstoppable hurry, live life in sips, tasting it, as if each moment was a holiday, like a continued, infinite pause... my existence.

I often go into the quietness of my heart, to take my restless mind to a calm, quiet, meditative state...

I waste a lot of time on redundant things, unnecessary stories. I transform this time into free minutes to dedicate to my personal growth, to increase my self-confidence, to things I enjoy and that help me advance...

I've finished industriously filling my agenda with things to avoid having time to make uncomfortable changes, things that would require effort...

I save time and energy by not thinking, doing or saying unnecessary things. The fastest way to finish trivial and superfluous activities is not to do them at all. That way I make free time to do things that I like without looking at the clock, without timing.

I lose a lot of time getting caught up in work that doesn't concern me, feeding people's egos, patting other people's backs, swelling up their cockiness just to collect their crumbs of esteem and admiration. Instead I can provide subtle praise, healing, for the person who really needs it and holds out their cup, empty of esteem.

I don't even lift a finger to show that I can do it best or that I'm right... unless it's needed.

I remove the following from my vocabulary: compare, compete, argue, judge, criticize, give unnecessary explanations...

Once in awhile, I'll read or mentally review *My Prodigious Changes List* so that they don't get put into the forgotten drawer.

These changes bring happiness to my life. They facilitate my personal advancement and brighten up my torch. They shake off the dust that's been sticking to me over the course of my life and awaken the precious being that I am with all the good I have inside of me.

Before I wasted time with my favorite preoccupations, and I left the things that I wanted to change until tomorrow.

I define some spaces to achieve some of my changes. Instead of jotting things down as "I'm going to spend some time reading", I write "I'm going to read for a while after meals." Instead of "I exercise everyday", I put "After getting up I am going to dedicate some time to practice yoga." That way, I won't finish the day not having done them, piled up, forgotten by the day's hustle and bustle.

I try to avoid being constantly busy and using up every minute of my time, because it might stress me out. I'm generous with my time. One of the reasons for *My Prodigious Changes* is to gain time to spend on my evolution, make my light brighter, discover myself, to do things I like, to feel life's gift... I reserve time to go at my own pace, free, relaxed, my own way, feeling how life passes by without any hurry or obligations, unoccupied, wandering, wasting time... gaining peace...

Some changes don't require any time to integrate, it's enough just to remember them, to want them, to have willpower... for example: *I wake up an hour earlier. I don't waste time arguing. I don't agree to do things I don't actually want to do. I give my stomach a break between meals, I don't snack. Goodbye tobacco and alcohol, my body will have a happy surprise.* With these changes, I actually gain time, money and energy.

I say my opinions without trying to convince others, not even myself as I could be wrong. In fact, as I move forward, Life changes my understanding of things, improving it, crossing things out and adding new ones. It has perfect vision, infinitely sharper than mine.

I don't bother explaining my projects, my activities, why I do the things I do, say what I say and think what I think. This decision saves a big chunk of my free time pie.

Generally, I don't give just to give, only when I feel it from the heart. I try not to waste my time wringing out ideas, turning them over and over, looking for the "perfect" gift to look good, to please others' ego... and my own. A lot of these gifts will, for lack of space, end up in the garbage. What a waste of money! The best gift is my friendship, my time, my love... from my heart's gift shop, a valuable gift that can't be found in any shopping centre.

I don't waste a gram of time or energy trying to prove my worth.

I don't get involved in arrogant arguments, banal questions, competitions... That way I won't get angry and I'll gain time and energy.

My master trick for generating more free time is to find and get rid of everything that I no longer have to think about, talk about or do because I've repeated it so many times already and it doesn't help me advance, instead it pulls me back...

Let's see what surprise messages I have on my answering machine. Before, it was always full of invitations which I didn't know how to refuse. I'd put them all in my agenda until it was overflowing with commitments. That left me without time and money to enjoy life and, instead of playing life's game, I had to fight against it and I became overwhelmed. Now that I don't answer the group's calls I can peacefully work on the translation, and on my personal growth.

"You have one new message." Let's see who it's from…

"Hey pal, I'm giving you the biggest news of the year: tomorrow night in my studio there's going to be a preview of my brilliant artistic talent. I'm showing my new paintings. Unparalleled in their magnificence. They'll blow you away. Bring your sunglasses. My new style will astonish you. Only for my closest friends and regular buyers. I'm going to see if I have more success selling in my studio. Bring something to eat and the necessary drinks to celebrate it. Don't even think about not coming, it'll be a great artistic event. Unbeatable. Spread the word amongst your wealthy friends, who could be potential buyers. Wear your sequinned dress to liven things up."

Me, wealthy friends? You're a bit clueless. Look, I'm sorry, but I'm not going.

Time to eat. What will I make myself today? Something simple, nutritious, tasty, quick to prepare and that doesn't need to go in a cooking pot or a frying pan. Heat destroys, deteriorating the nutrients. I know: celery, carrots, and apples cut into little pieces with some olive oil or virgin sesame oil and a pinch of sea salt with millet or quinoa and seaweed. Since I stopped hanging out with the group, I've gone back to preparing natural food, which lightens my body.

Eat, eat… Food, having you keeps us in constant movement. Before, it was about going after the prey with a bow and arrow. Now, the bow and arrow has changed into a computer and a mouse and the prey's become the monthly paycheck. The necessary requirement to pay for food and shelter.

Food, I dedicate so much of my day, my life to you. I could grow so much during the time I spend earning money to pay for you, cooking you, eating you, digesting you, washing the dishes... It takes up so much of my time and energy that I could be using to study languages, read, run... do so many things instead of exercising my jaws, but I have to eat. What I can do is simplify the process, reduce all that time. Eat wisely, just enough to be well nourished. Have less junk in the kitchen. Prepare simpler foods. Fruit is fast, peel and eat, the banana is a great invention. Carrots, zucchini, tomatoes. Almonds are easy to eat and they give me calcium.

I'm more and more careful of the food I put in my body, choosing the healthiest, and I only eat what I need to stay fit and healthy. That way, I don't go around half-asleep all day, wasting my energy digesting food. Instead I'll use it on things I need to do. I'll be smart and not gorge myself with incompatible foods that lengthen my digestion, holding oxygen in my stomach that should be in my head creating beautiful ideas.

I used to mix sweet and acidic fruits, not knowing that they were incompatible. I walked around all day bloated and uncomfortable. I have fruit in the morning. I've read that eating fruit after a meal is not recommended, except apples, which are considered neutral.

I've gotten used to spacing meals out from each other to give my stomach time to finish digesting before it receives another load of work. Long, slow digestions tire my body and mind. They give my face a fatigued expression and my eyes become weary. Heavy foods slow down my body's vibration.

Grandma's healthy food books are opening my eyes. She always said: "Evi, you are what you eat." They're helping me update the healthy diet she got me used to, which I'd forgotten when I was with the group. They stuffed themselves with junk food. They didn't worry about it at all, making fun of me for being careful with what I ate. In the end, I got tired of their jokes and criticisms and I ate the same things they ate. I forgot my principles.

If I had communicated with one of my millions of cells when I went out with the group, I'd have probably heard:

"I work for you, Eva. My workday is 24 hours a day, 365 days a year. I have a complaint: you're choking me with your tobacco smoke, with your alcoholic drinks, with your junk food… If you keep going like this, without taking care of me, I'll get sick. I love you… even though you've never thanked me for working for you."

"I'm sorry cell, my friend, you're totally right. My deepest gratitude, from the bottom of my heart, goes to you and your millions of friends for taking care of my body… our body. Thanks to it, my spirit can continue learning its lessons on this blue planet. As an apology, I'll play some relaxing music to fill you with their pacifying energy. I'll hum along as I'm listening. I'll improve my voice. I hope you enjoy it."

"I love you, my beloved body. From now on, I'll say it to you more often. I know that every time you hear it, it makes you healthier and younger."

Enough with the translation, my eyes are tired. I'm going to put on some music and let myself be taken in by its rhythm. Let's see what I put on… This is a good one.

I'm setting you free, my dear body, move as you please, massaging and balancing the organs where I have blocked energy with your healing movements. I'm giving you the control, you're giving the directions. You know the matter better than I do, I'm just your partner. What great songs, what pleasure! They lift my spirit. It's a great exercise for my body and soul.

I have a message, let's see who it's from…

"Hi, Eva, it's Isa. I don't have money, again. I can't seem to manage my expenses. My neighbors have been nice enough to offer me the hallway cleaning job, but even so, it's not enough. How about a trade? You baby-sit for me in exchange for an unlimited number of croquettes, the ones you like. It'd be for next Saturday night. Let me know. Kisses. Take care."

Of course I will. Only two days left until the croquettes feast, they're the best in the world, and her baby is an angel.

Instead of always thinking about what I don't have, I should look at all the things that I do have and thank life for them. Why don't I do it now? This is a good time to be thankful.

Thank you to those who are wiser than me. Thank you for all the times that you have walked beside me, acting as my mirror, showing me what I can improve in myself, even if it hurts. That way I can also be a good example for others.

Thank you ancestors. I've reached my current evolution due to your determination. All of your efforts, your will to change, to learn, to improve your mind and body, have been sent to me through genetic mail.

Thank you Life for having marked in my heart what's valuable for me, regardless of its market value. No barcodes. Value can't be measured by the sound of its clinking. The best things in life are free: the smell and beauty of a flower, feeling a breeze's gentle touch, a look of recognition…

Thank you elevator. You saved me from walking up nine flights of stairs when I twisted my foot. And now that I'm passing by the doorman, I'll thank him too… No, no I can't, it's beyond me, I still can't stand him. I'll do it next time, maybe by then I will have gotten over it…

"Good morning, Miss Eva. You've got a …"

I left him with his words in his mouth. He was going to make one of those nasty comments that make me angry, but I breezed past him quickly. His jokes, his stupid behavior and cynical comments make my stomach turn, I can't stand them. In any case, thank you Life for giving me the doorman as a lesson, I know that it's to test my patience and bad moods. He's the thermometer that measures the degrees of my intolerance.

Now it looks like we're getting along better, since the water bucket incident. He's still drying himself off. I couldn't stop myself. Since then he's been much more cautious with what he says to me.

He thinks twice before speaking when he can control his mocking nature and his desire to interfere.

I woke up crying, emotional… Tonight I've had two wonderful dreams!

In front of me appeared a being surrounded by a shining aura. On its shoulder there was a white dove. With its index finger it created a star in the air, which radiated golden sparkle. The dove took the star in its beak, fluttered over me and placed the star gently on my head. Energy ran through my body, awakening my strength.

The second dream was also very emotional. A metallic gold convertible was parked in front of me and a man got out, grabbing a bouquet of yellow daisies from the back seat. He approached me and offered them to me. The large size of the bouquet obscured his face. I felt his waves of love, how his spirit warmly embraced mine. I could read his thoughts: "We'll see each other soon. There will be four of us. I love you, Eva."

The phone's ringing, it's Ros' number.

"Hi, Ros."

"Hi, Eva. Look, I'm calling to see if you could babysit my kids tonight from eight until, maybe, two. I've got a big date, I'm like a little girl with a new toy. I'll tell you later because I've got dinner on the stove and the kids are really excited."

"Yes, I can do that. I'll be there at eight until you get home."

"You can have dinner here. I'll make you something delicious that you'll really like."

"Okay, my mouth's watering already. Don't worry too much if you're in a hurry. A sandwich would be fine."

"Don't worry, I've got plenty of time. See you later Eva, and thanks."

"See you later, Ros."

Ros is such a wonderful person, and her kids are lovely.

I'm going to practice focusing my mind, directing my thoughts towards one topic, my inner warrior:

My inner warrior is full of strength. She is in my heart, ready to continue advancing along paths full of light, virtue, wisdom…

My inner warrior grows with my daily activity from the smallest to the biggest event. She doesn't need to isolate herself on a mountaintop hermitage. It's within our daily environment that she faces her biggest challenges. She has her biggest trials at work, with family, friends, and the infinite lessons that come up during the course of the day. They're inner and outer victories. Victories full of love, because of love and for love.

My warrior's goals are: increase my inner peace, my tolerance and understanding, my serenity in chaotic and difficult situations, my level of consciousness, my mental strength and serenity, my truths and also: decrease my judgements, attachments, impatience, fears, hurries…

My warrior doesn't turn off her principles, nor does she cede her power to appease and please others.

My warrior has prepared her "No, thank you" and she maintains it shiny and ready to be used as many times as needed and whenever she feels like using it.

My warrior has a pass to navigate through the iridescent landscapes of my Inner Universe, full of its peace and wisdom. Why don't I focus more on getting closer to them? Because I don't know what I'm missing out on. Because it's hard for me to control my thoughts. Because it's easier for me to sit in the back seat and let my old, monotonous thoughts drive, taking me where they want, instead of facing them and choosing myself. Because I spend the day moving useless things around and I go to bed without having dedicated even five minutes to the marvelous mental quieting that allows me to lower my mind to my heart. I'll keep trying. I won't give up.

My warrior becomes stronger in my home oasis by meditating, and by battling against those thoughts and rushes which have always subjugated me.

And next, it wouldn't be a bad idea if I said a few positive affirmations, letting myself rock to my gentle breathing, feeling the air's warm love caress my chest. I breathe in. *My warrior is waking up.* I exhale. *My warrior is waking up.* Inhale. *My warrior is waking up.* I'll change. *My warrior is awake.* It's better that way. *My warrior is awake...*

I'm going to have some green tea... My grandma gave me this mug. My nostalgia emerges. I'm not going to cry because I know we aren't separated. I'm getting more and more of her messages through my dreams. I know that she's happy where she is and that she wants me to be happy here. I know that our spirits are connected, and that physically we'll meet again from time to time, at different points along the eternal paths of our existences.

I learned so much from my grandma. She always paid attention to me when I wanted her to. I would snuggle up on the sofa while listening to her, and she would sit in her wicker chair...

"Evi, a person's real worth doesn't have anything to do with whether they're tall or short, if they have a big or a small nose, if they wear luxurious or worn, old-fashioned clothes, nor if they're skinny or fat, nor even if they're immensely wealthy or extremely poor. These details are superfluous. They're insignificant external details and aren't worth anything if they're compared with the real value. The real value is hard to see because it's in the heart. Remember, measure people by the love they have in their hearts."

"Grandma, I like elephants a lot and I don't care if they have thick legs, enormous bodies and long trunks. I like giraffes with their long necks."

"Do you love me even though I'm fat?"

"Of course I do, grandma. I love you so much, so, so much that I can't love you anymore. The love in your heart is very, very big."

"Do you know why you love me so much? Because your heart is full of love, it only sees what's beautiful in me. What others see as ugliness, you transform into beauty just as you do with the elephant's trunk."

"Grandma, I don't like lions, tigers or crocodiles because they eat gazelles. I don't understand why they can't eat leaves and grass like gorillas and elephants and rhinos and horses and giraffes and... and cows."

"Their bodies are different. Maybe they can't digest grass. Would you like some toast with plum jam?"

"Yes, I'd like that very much. Grandma, you explain things to me in such a fun way, like a story..."

I miss those evenings we spent together, when grandma's desire to teach me fed pearls of wisdom to my insatiable curiosity. The truth is that I would drown her with a lot of questions that popped out of my head, faster than popcorn. She was very patient with me. I didn't stop. I would ask her about everything.

"Grandma, it's been days since you've given me some trick to be happy."

"Okay, my love, I'll give you the best trick of all: Be Love and love, unconditionally, without asking for anything in return."

When I lost grandma, I found myself lost, I kept myself to myself. I lost the ability to surprise myself. Loneliness snowed over me, covering my will to live. I stopped smelling the flowers' fragrance, whistling when I woke up, singing during the day, contemplating the stars... It silenced my inner child's desire to play. Grandma's love stimulated all of that, which got rid of my sorrows. When she flew away, a lot of the little lights that she kept lit inside of me were put out by my sadness.

I'm a Universe Nomad

I'm tired of going at full speed, I don't want to run anymore. I'm going to switch trotting for a calm pace.

Deceitful hurries, I'm going to take advantage of this retreat imposed on me by the translation to confront you, to trade you for peace and tranquility. It's going to be difficult for me. You're deeply rooted, but I'll make an effort.

Because of you, hurries, I forget about looking up at the stars, I look at flowers without seeing them, I miss the chance of feeling the velvet breeze against my skin. I push aside feeling. I only run. Hurries, I no longer want you with me.

Because of you, hurries, I don't realize that my life is a quick escape from my monotonous and repetitive mental labyrinths. I live vertiginously, looking without seeing, fleeting, passing by, with eyes half-asleep, without stopping to taste what I see… Life. The never-ending attack of miniscule rancid things hides what's essential for me. My ego takes advantage of my confusion. It controls me, inciting me to arrive and be in everything so that it can show off its extravagant galas.

Because of you, hurries, I go faster. I've sped up my pace. I don't know how to be calm in my urban nest without desiring the noisy street and people's chatter. Hurries, you control me. You push me without giving me a break. Honestly, I don't want you with me anymore.

I don't like looking back and seeing so many wasted pleasures, so many wonderful things gone up in smoke, unnoticed, lost to me because of my accelerated lifestyle. Hurries, take note, I no longer want your company. Get out of my life. I want to slow down my crazy race towards nowhere, that forces me to wear glasses that don't allow me to see, and earmuffs that don't allow me to hear. Why am I still running? My time will not run out. I have all the time in the world. I'm eternal. What quickens my pace? What do I want to get to so quickly? What makes me push myself to reach for goals that I don't need and to achieve success that I don't want? Why am I trying to impress others? To receive their admiration? To convince myself that I'm worth it?

These achievements leave me empty. They're fleeting. They're only patches. I sense that my efforts are to heal the wounds from that time when somebody or some people rejected my love, filling me with disaffection and loneliness. Not getting their love left me deeply marked. I was left with the cup that I put before them to fill with love, empty. Since then, I've been longing to fill it. Time hasn't erased that scar of rejection, it's still alive. I run after people trying to diminish it…

I want to change the way I live life. Live as if time didn't go by, as if the hands on the clock didn't move, without calendars or schedules that hasten my hurry. And I want, want, want to stop in my path when my feelings call upon my heart. And when life grants me those unexpected marvelous moments, full of emotion, fascination, sentiment, passion, fervor, excitement, enthusiasm, poetry… I will stop in my path and live the moment with all my senses.

I want to stop treating life like a never-ending list of obstacles that bother me and that I must do quickly, without stopping to rest. I want to live it like an adventure, an amusement, a game… like children do. Keeping all of my attention on the game, on what I'm doing, letting it happen without any effort, without tension, without comparing and judging myself, without precipitations. Submerging, transforming myself into the game. Playing for pleasure, not for the desire to win or to do it perfectly, or to receive applauses and cheers.

I'll no longer over-pack my agenda with unnecessary obligations. I'll reserve time for emotions, laughter, humor, for my sensitivity, my humanity… I'll often take my inner child out for a walk. She has been punished, facing the wall, for a long time now.

I'll no longer run around doing things to convince others and myself that I'm worth something. Of course I'm valuable and deserve to be happy and enjoy things, I'm a more precious being than I think I am.

I'm very happy with the friendship I have with Ros. She's such a positive person who radiates modesty and nobility. She's so true to herself, to what she feels. Life has been hard on her, but she perseveres. She maintains her enthusiasm and keeps going… She's serving as a mirror for me, which shows me the changes I need to integrate.

I used to make an effort rummaging around in my purse of trivialities, forgetting what's authentic, the truth. I'm getting closer, finding logic in things that I couldn't understand before. I'm discovering beauty, qualities in others, in myself, in everything, that I didn't notice before.

My goals are clearer: increase my consciousness, my Love energy, travel along a path of light to Light, enjoy the beauty of Life…

What laziness! What sleepiness! I would love to just stay in bed, but I'm going to get up. I don't want the translation deadline to arrive and not be finished with it.

Last night's dream is still in my head. I was in a house, trying to open the door to go out, but the key wouldn't fit in the lock. A man appeared, the only thing I remember about his face was that he had a friendly smile. He offered me a magic wand. I touched the door with it and it opened. A paradise full of flowers, birds, butterflies, exotic trees and blue skies riding over infinite mountains appeared before my eyes. What does it mean? Maybe that I'm locked into my sadness and, suddenly, my heart and mind will open themselves up to happiness.

Okay, up. I can hear the little birds' from the square. They're my alarm clock. It's such a bright day, it encourages me to live. I'm going to start the day off with my evolutionary exercises. I'll start with some breathing exercises and yoga, followed by a meditation. They'll leave a trail of peace and serenity that will last throughout the day.

Oh! I almost forgot I had the dream about the rock, again! But there was a change. I could see the enormous rock from afar and there was someone on top of it with their arms open, greeting the sun. Clouds passed by quickly. The wind shook her tunic with fury. I ran, ran as fast as I could. I got to the rock completely exhausted, but with all of my strength, I leapt and landed standing in front of the person who was there. It was me! We slowly walked toward each other, recognizing and hugging each other. The dream ended right there and then.

I don't get attached to places. I'm a Universe nomad. It's my house. I don't store and collect things. I save, keep feelings and experiences, which I carry in my backpack of stars, they don't weigh me down. I fly free of burdens, like the bird that only carries its coat of feathers, its songs, its great desire for living, its feelings...

There are a lot of unnecessary things that enslave me: rules, labels, diplomas, appearances, prejudices, styles, gadgets... I'll try to detach myself from them. Oh, I've forgotten three important ones: the sense of urgency that's always harassing me, my frequent sorrows and my boastful and arrogant personal image, my ego, that's always preening in front of the mirror.

I can put up my tent anywhere and at any time. My calming oasis travels with me, it can be found in my Inner Universe, always ready to take me in its warm embrace of love and peace.

Life tells me: "Here you go, I'm giving you some time. You choose how to use it. Here you go, here's some money. You choose how to spend it. Here you go, take some vital energy. You choose how to use it. I won't charge you interest or give you conditions."

Life gives me a job to do and says: "Do it as you wish." It doesn't order me around as if I were a puppet. It gives me free will and hands me over the responsibility. If anyone is going to stop me, it's going to be me. Even though I usually blame all of my mistakes and failures on Life and others.

Life tells me: "I give you liberty. It's possible that you won't use it wisely and that you'll lose it, that's how you'll learn. You know that you can get it back at any time, it's always inside you. I'll always speak to you in a language you can understand, on your current level of consciousness. As you develop, I'll intensify your lessons. And remember, if you don't get along with me, it's because you want to change me. When you can accept me as I am, and realize that you're the one who has to change, you'll feel a lot better and happier."

I've got it all clear. I'm going to live as if I were painting a picture. My life's painting. I've got the canvas in front of me. Its blank surface is waiting for my creation. Who's going to paint it, me or everyone else? Do I hand the brush over for some pats on the back, for some grains of affection? It's my choice. I can paint what I want, what I feel, without worrying about pleasing others with what they would like to see. No one is forcing me. No one moves my hand or my heart. Maybe they're trying: the merchants, the critics, the public, the galleries, my comfort in doing what I'm used to, my ego's eccentricity... I won't give up my power. I choose. I choose. I choose. I paint from my heart for my Inner Me, for the Universe. I can choose happy or sad colors, it's my decision. I'm the creator of my circumstances. I shape my reality with my own brushstrokes, my thoughts, words and actions.

I can keep myself in chains or be free as a bird. I can change at any moment, spread a layer of paint over what's already on the canvas and start again. I can change whatever I want, even the style. It can be figurative, abstract, pointillist, surrealist, impressionist, cubist... I can paint with a brush, my fingers, a broom or digitally with a mouse. I let a brushstroke fall upon the canvas. The color! It's fantastic! I let myself go...

I let my feelings guide me, they've been locked up inside of me for such a long time. It's about time! I paint for pleasure. I'm careful not to splatter those who are painting around me and their canvases. It's their space of freedom.

And if I want, I can stop reflecting on my amazing painting and go to eat an apple and listen to my favorite music.

And later, I'll leave my flat. Done! Today I'll take a day off, go out, and walk around aimlessly, to stretch my legs. I'll take my backpack with something to eat: a banana, some bread with oil, almonds, mineral water... I can walk along the sea front, go to a park, look at galleries, bookshops ... We'll see...

Oh, I'm having such a great time! I needed some fresh air. It's so beautiful! Sunbeams reflect off the waves, making infinite reflective sparkles. If I look at them with my eyes half-closed the effect is even more spectacular.

What a pretty shell! It's wonderful walking along the shore feeling the cool caress of the water on my feet. I think it's releasing the static electricity from my body, that sometimes stings me and makes it difficult for me to sleep. My grandma got me used to wearing only cotton clothes, it's static-free. I'm going to stretch out on the sand to feel the sun caressing my body accompanied by the murmur of the waves...

I'm going to take some time to reflect. I'm going to scold my false ego: I'm sick of you, presumptuous ego, of your impositions, your orders and mandates, your demands... From now on, you're going to find things a lot harder, something has changed. Now you're not only challenging me, you're also challenging my inner warrior's strength. Time has matured me. You've been playing with me, using me like a fool, a puppet and a chauffeur so that I'd take you out to show off your designer clothes. Say goodbye to all of that.

Ego, I'm tired of looking through the narrow-vision telescope you put before my eyes. You turn it around so that it only focuses on you.

You wear bells and sound the alarm to tell everyone you're coming, to capture the entire world's attention and put yourself in the center, making a lot of fuss, causing the same spectacle as always.

Little ego, you enjoy dominating my attention and everyone else's, managing my emotions and making me spend time buffing you so that you can be seen from far away. You love showing off and dazzling people.

But, your time of arrogant preposterousness is coming to an end. Now my awareness has grown and has exposed your tricks. I can see you coming. You can start packing your bags.

"You have a new message."

"What's wrong with you? Why aren't you answering? Get out of your prehistoric lethargic mood. Pick-up the phone and call me."

You're still as classy, diplomatic and patient as ever.

I'm going to take a break from Ric's translation. I'll give myself a silent break. What kind of silence should I choose? There are so many types of silence: Caressing silence. Screaming silence. Healing silence. Marginalizing silence. Joyful silence. Disappointing silence. Forgetful silence. Painful silence. Ecstatic Silence. Respectful silence. Scared silence. Bored silence. Flashy silence. Smiley silence.

I choose the silence from my heart's love. I choose the silence that moves me forward. I choose the silence that helps me. I choose the silence that brings me closer to the truth. I choose the silence that quiets my mind. I choose the silence from my soul's states that bring me closer to the Universe's pulse. I choose the silence that allows me to listen to a bird's laugh, the sea's words, the breeze's secrets, the tree's whispers. I choose the silence that puts me in touch with my Inner Presence. I choose the silence that shares love from a silent heart.

This is a very lucid dream, I recognize that I'm dreaming, but it happened, is happening or will happen. When I wake up I'll probably have forgotten it or I'll think it was only a fantasy. I'm up in a high place, surrounded by a lot of people in an impressive silence. They don't take their eyes off me. They're waiting for something important... my voice. I begin to speak, my words flow without effort. I only provide the voice. Someone is dictating the words to me...

Ros

I arrive ten minutes early so that she won't have to rush. The doorbell isn't working. I'll bang on the door really hard, because with all the noise the kids make, they won't hear otherwise.

"Hi, Eva. Great, you're so punctual. You look good."

"You too, Ros. Wow, Iren, you look pretty. You're the prettiest girl in the world, and you two have grown a lot and you're so good-looking! It's so nice to see you all together. What a lovely wall, full of photos, letters, drawings… They weren't there before."

"It's to show the progress of the projects that the kids and I donate to. These are the photos of the child we sponsor, from when he was little until now where he's eleven. We get a letter from him every year with a photo and a drawing that he does for us. It's a really effective NGO, they do good work. They have a website where you click on the project you're contributing towards and you can see photos of the progress they're making. We know where and whom our small donation is going to, which strengthens our bond.

I download and print the photos with the kids' help and then we hang them in chronological order. This is the story of the little village we're sponsoring: this one is from when they started building the school. Here's another one, with many of the villagers in it, it is from the inauguration day. Here they're building a rain water reservoir so they can water their orchards, vegetables and other things. They're stopping the growth of the desert by refertilising the land."

"They look so happy."

"Yes, they're fantastic. This photo is from when they installed a potable water system. Here they're putting the roof on a tiny health center. This is a little refuge shelter for the street kids."

"Their smiles are so full of light. What a pretty box! So colorful, with such an evocative phrase: "I'm a smile creator." There's a list next to it: Cinema, snack, toy…

"It's a foldable moneybox. Information on the project is written on the outside of the box. The kids call it the *magic box* because it makes the dream that's printed on it come true. It's just a piece of standard-sized poster board that the kids put together really easily. They folded along the dotted lines, removed the protective strip, stuck the sides together and it was ready to hold our spontaneous contributions."

"Spontaneous contributions?"

"Yes, when we feel like it, we put some of our spending money into these aid projects. We put it in the little *magic box*. We mark the quantity down on this list, and, every once in awhile, we read it. It's satisfying to see how a small quantity, from time to time, increases little by little. When I go by the bank, I deposit the money into the NGO's account for this project.

It's a way for the kids, tomorrow's adults, to realize that there are people who are going through hard times and that helping them is an act of humanity.

One afternoon, I invited them to the movies. While waiting in line the youngest one said, "Mommy, let's be smile creators. Let's go to the park instead and put the money from the entrance tickets into the box for the village. Do you want to?" The other two agreed and applauded the idea. It's an impulse we feel sometimes, and we put it into action.

The idea often comes from the kids: "Kids, do you want an ice cream?" "I don't. This afternoon I'm going to be a smile creator." That time, the other two played deaf. They had their eyes and stomachs set on the ice cream, and they decided not to be smile creators. I've got to run, or else I'm going to be late for my date. In the fridge you'll find what I made for dinner. I hope you like it."

"Of course I will. Good luck on your date."

"Thanks, I'll need it. He's the ideal guy for me, he gets along well with the kids. I'm going to let my feelings flow from my heart."

"Hi, Eva. Sorry for coming back so late."

"You look so happy, your face is glowing."

"Look."

"What a beautiful ring!"

"He's asked me to marry him."

"Ahhh! Congratulations, Ros!"

"I see that you've built a small fence in the kitchen door's entrance."

"Yes, I put it there so that the kids wouldn't go in. Kitchens are dangerous for children."

"You're very aware of preventing accidents."

"Yes, my mother was very cautious and I've inherited it from her. This small fence is the same one I had when I was child. I was able to avoid the hazards of frying pans that stuck out... My big dream is to set-up a shop for expecting mothers, babies and kids, but I haven't started it because I don't have enough money. I've got it well planned out.

I could sell using an online catalogue and save myself the rent and the shop maintenance, but I'm drawn to having a shop, dealing directly with people. I could publicize it by putting flyers in mailboxes and in the neighborhood shops. I could design and print them myself at home.

It wouldn't be about making lots of money. I'd be happy just to cover my expenses. The idea is to help, advise families about the great changes that a baby in the house brings in terms of food, security, infant healthcare, furniture, cotton clothes, pacifiers, having a safe box to keep tiny things locked away because at that age babies put everything in their mouths, strollers, safe cribs, proper utensils meant to minimize risks to babies and children...

I could sell books about this issue with clear, easy and simple information. It would be a place where people would be welcomed and attended to, where they could find information without any kind of purchasing pressure. I enjoy helping people, being useful to others."

"It's a wonderful project. It sounds very interesting. It's a good idea."

"If you're interested, we could go in on it together, if you could bring in half of the remaining money, which is what is stopping the project, we could split the profits and each only works half a day."

"Your offer is very tempting. I love children so much. Okay, I'll do it, business partner. In a few months, I'm getting paid a sum of money and then we can start to do the numbers and see if our funds will be enough. I'll call you when I have the money."

"I'm so happy that you've accepted!"

"Get moving. Let's see if you can find a decent and cosy shop with a low rent."

"I'm already on it. I've seen some that I think we could afford, although the rents are generally sky-high. We'd be okay with a small space, we could sell a lot of the merchandise through a catalogue without having them in the shop…'"

I'll surprise Ric, by giving him the translation as a finished book. I'll work a bit on the cover's digital design, I'll transfer the photos I've taken to the computer, and with them I'll make a collage and put it through some artistic filters. It's creative work and I'll have fun at the same time. The mouse becomes the painter's magic brush. "I'll change this background color", click, and it's done, almost as fast as you could think it. No more tubes of paint, brushes. Nothing to clean-up.

Technology's magic is simplifying things, changing lifestyles. It's a shame not to have an evolutionary mouse to change my habits with just a click. I have it within myself. It's my Inner Wisdom. It's only half activated.

The idea I had that meditating was a waste of time has been replaced by the certainty that it's very important for my personal development. Practicing meditation is changing my life. It's straightforward and simple, but not easy. Your attention and thoughts are as elusive and slippery as a fish, but it's worth it because it's bringing a lot of improvements into my life:

It increases my peace, energy, perception and allows my Inner Wisdom to have a receptive mental space, free of thoughts. This mental state enables me to receive the answers to my questions and clues to show me the way I should follow.

It helps me live more in the present. I used to look without seeing. I heard without listening. I vaguely knew what the movie was about. My mind wandered, absent from what was happening, dividing itself between yesterday and tomorrow, forgetting about the present. Now, I see what I'm looking at, listen to what I hear and I'm living in the present with a wider perception that comes from my heart.

It opens the door for my Inner Wisdom that helps my creativity, my artistic talent, my poetic side, my genius flow...

It helps me take my mind to my heart's quiet oasis, maintaining it quiet, mute, available, so that I can look inside, get closer to the truths, within earshot of what my Inner Wisdom is transmitting to me, filling me with its strength, intuition, knowledge...

It increases my self-confidence, my detachment, and diminishes my fears and the time I spend hurrying.

It helps me to keep out thoughts that distort reality, to focus my attention, my comprehension, and to delve deeper into what I am contemplating.

It helps me decrease and control my exaggerated angry reactions when things don't go as I want them to, when people criticize me or underestimate me.

It balances, harmonizes, and calms me. If there's peace inside of me, I'll also have it outside. My inner changes are projected out and influence the exterior. Anywhere I am, I emit peace and love to others, to the earth, to the Universe.

It establishes a state of peace that allows me to observe my ideas, words and actions, giving them the red or green light.

It makes my mind strong by not allowing any of those thoughts that crowd around its entrance door to go through. They're surprised to find it shut, never having seen it that way before, and with the sign: "We reserve the right to refuse entry." They don't back away. They don't accept the rule. Again and again, they tear the door down and burst in with their ruckus, messing up my mental peace. Meditation provides me with the strength necessary to reinforce that door.

While I meditate I'm quiet, I give my thoughts, words and actions a vacation. Once I've finished, I'm in a relaxed and peaceful state that lasts throughout the day. It's helping me evolve, expanding my consciousness, integrating the changes that I'm yet to achieve, and increasing my strength, making it easier to confront my daily difficulties.

A Real Dream

I can see grandma coming this way, she's so smiley.

"Hi, dear Eva. Once again we find each other in the ethereal space of dreams."

"Hi, grandma! I'm so happy that we're able to get in touch this way! Why didn't you communicate with me earlier? When you left, I was so alone."

"I couldn't. I'm in another dimension. It's not like talking to your neighbor where you knock on the door and she opens it. I called on you many times, but you couldn't hear the bell. You had to change your frequency to be able to receive me. Now you can hear me in your dreams, but in the future you'll be able to do so when you're awake, during the day. I've been protecting you from here, guiding you when I have been able to. I've never left you. I've always been watching how things were going for you, helping you many times without you noticing it.

Also, we haven't communicated earlier so as not to interfere with your development and the lessons you still had to learn. The path you have taken on your own has made you more mature. It has increased your strength, your capacity to reflect and be silent."

"My heart has been through a lot of pain, I've had so many difficulties. I've missed you so much."

"On earth, it's hard to understand that difficulties are opportunities, lessons that life puts in front of us to help us develop ourselves. People tend to think of them as punishments, bad luck, misfortune, problems... you need to have a wider scope that allows you to see the good side, instead of focusing only on the negative."

"Grandma, tell me what you're doing now in the place where you're living."

"I am continuing to learn. I have a lot of opportunities to help me keep growing here. From this dimension we can help people, even though there are some who reject the lifesaver. Then, we can't intervene. We aren't allowed to overrule free will.

Here, there aren't relatives or families. It's as if we were all friends, companions. We've been meeting each other in different lives with different roles like neighbors, children, partners, siblings, parents, enemies, friends… I'm also preparing the missions and lessons for my next life on earth."

"Will it be soon? Will we find each other again?"

"I'd like that very much. The guides that are helping me plan everything still haven't decided where and when my next destination will be."

"What's it like where you are?"

"It's a beautiful place with colors and sounds that don't exist on earth, that are richer…"

"What's the dimension called?"

"Well, you can call it our house because it's really our home. After every adventure on earth, we return here."

"You're so young grandma. Younger than when I was a child."

"On this dimension you can choose the age that you're more comfortable with. Your body isn't as dense, as heavy. You lose matter, but you gain spiritual substance. You can barely feel gravity, it's different here. At a higher consciousness, greater lightness. My spiritual body is younger, lighter. The surroundings are different, but similar to the earth's. There is a very special light that illuminates everything, that feeds and nourishes.

The ego, with its old habits, disappears. Love penetrates everything. It's omnipresent. The influence that pride, envy, ambition, competition and fear have on earth leaves, allowing your mind to be full of love, silence, transparency, far more awake and perceptive."

"Getting older is a pain, grandma, you get wrinkly and sick."

"The soul doesn't have wrinkles or illnesses. The main reason for going to earth isn't to be on magazine covers with a model's body, but to increase one's consciousness and achieve a loving heart. You can get that at any age, also, if you fervently desire it, during your transition."

"Why don't my relationships last?"

"Because you think that they'll end, that they'll leave you. You don't enjoy them while they last, but suffer through them. You want some assurance that they'll last forever because you suffer a lot when they abandon you. You don't want to risk being rejected, so, unconsciously, you break off the relationship, ruin it. To make a long story short, before getting to the top, you're already thinking of the way down. It's an unconscious reaction that comes from some disaffection that you suffered a long time ago. Don't ask me what, I can't tell you more. Life will reveal it to you soon."

"Okay, grandma. What have I accomplished up to now? Nothing, not for me or for others."

"Eva, you haven't noticed, but you've spread a lot of good around you. You have a big heart, but when your strong personality and your bad attitude come out, you hide it."

"As much as I've meditated about my life, I can't think of anything good."

"Look, there was a very bitter period in my life. Depression took control of my life. I was very isolated. Not much earlier, I'd lost my husband, and that was added to the loss of my daughter, your mother, which affected me a lot. Then, you came. You were a precious baby and brought a breath of fresh air to my life. Your desire to live awakened mine. You needed so much love and tenderness. You got rid of my drowsiness and helped me forget my sadness and defeats. Taking care of you made me feel useful, needed. Your never-ending curiosity, your clear gaze, so new and full of innocence, truth, purity and love reconciled me with life. How many times have you babysat for your friends for free?"

"Well, I'd take something from the fridge. It was a trade."

"How many times have you filled your elderly patients with smiles, love and hope? How many times have you listened to them patiently and with understanding? Your whole life is full of beautiful actions. Without knowing it, you've sown many seeds of love. What happens is that you demand too much of yourself and your inferiority complex lowers your self-esteem. Soon, you'll discover its cause and it'll disappear."

I'm awake, what a shame. Grandma was so young, so radiant, and so full of love, and I was interested in what she was saying. I'm going back to sleep to try to dream of her again. I'll send her a message: "I want to keep dreaming of you, grandma"... My eyes are closing... yes, I'm falling asleep... I can see her...

"Hi, grandma!"

"Good, Eva. You've wished hard enough and you've gotten what you wanted. Let's continue with our real dream. Your spatial antennae are expanding. In a short time, you'll be able to hear me directly."

"That'll be fantastic! You know, I felt so special when I was little and you called me Little Princess. It sounded like music from the stars."

"Now, my Little Princess has grown-up, which is why I've got a new name for you. I hope you like it."

"What is it?"

"Eva Luz."

"I love it! It's very special. I like the change."

"When you think of me, do it joyfully. Don't cry for me. In this place I'm okay, as you are on Earth. We don't need to make ourselves sad. Besides, we're in touch with our telepathic instant messaging. We need to be happy in our respective dimensions until we finish the time we've chosen to stay."

"Yes, grandma. I won't cry for you." I'm falling away from my sleep, again...

Now it's not so hard for me to control my thoughts while I meditate. I'm moving ahead. In time, if I keep it up, I'll be able to achieve it. It's still difficult to dedicate some time each day to practice it. I think I manage, instinctively, to fill the whole day with tasks so that I don't have a moment left to meditate.

Each time, I feel more comfortable practicing it. It makes me feel a special state of peace. My legs have gotten used to the lotus position without hurting or feeling uncomfortable anymore, and this makes my relaxation easier and the quality of my meditation better.

Why don't I practice more? I spend the day doing insignificant things and forget the fundamental things, like meditating. If I dedicated more time to it, I'd be able to manage my thoughts, my problems and my life better... It was a good idea to have a set time to meditate.

It's time to climb. I'll put one more sparkle inside my invisible backpack of stars. I'm going to say some positive affirmations, the exercise will serve as meditation, too. Lotus position. Close my eyes. I relax my mind and loosen my body. I lengthen my breath a little, not forcing it, gently, to pacify me, to help focus my attention.

Action. Let see how it works...

Inhaling. *I have positive thoughts.* Exhaling. *I have positive thoughts.* Inhaling. *I have positive thoughts.* Exhaling. *I have positive thoughts. I have positive thoughts. I have positive thou...* My back itches! It reminds me of the gorilla in the documentary I saw yesterday and how he scratched himself. I have to return it, it's overdue... My attention wanders off very easily, come on, again, lets start again, I'll change affirmation.

Inhaling. *I have an abundant economy.* Exhaling. *I have an abundant economy. I have an abundant economy.* I'm repeating it like a little parrot, not thinking about what I'm actually saying. This isn't doing me any good. I have to want it. It has to come from my heart and I need to focus my attention on it. Let's go, slower this time, calmly. I'll change the affirmation. *I'm happy... I'm happy... I'm happy... I'm happy...* I've forgotten to turn on the alarm for seven... *I'm happy...* I might forget to go and take care of Francis. I'm excited by the happiness she greets me with... I'll change affirmation: *My mind is quiet... My mind is quiet... My mind is quiet...* The phone is ringing. It could be someone from the group, they're still calling. I'll find out later when I listen to the messages. I'm glad that I stuck with my decision not to go out with them anymore. They asked me so many questions that I got a sore throat from giving them so many explanations. I've changed, no more explanations. Everyone has their own life. We each are the way we are. "What'll you do?" "I don't know, we'll see." "Why do you eat that way?" "It's just how I eat" and that's it.

Once again, my attention has flown away. When I'm distracted, one idea is quickly replaced by another. I know where I am when I start to think, but I don't know where I'll end up. Today, my mind is very turbulent. I'll stop affirmations' practice... I've been missing the baker's smile for awhile...

I spend a lot of my day sitting down. I'll put my friend the Singer of Truths on. I can listen to her while I walk up and down the hallway with good posture. Walking moves my heart, my ideas and balances my body's posture. Here's her radio station...

"Good morning, friends. My heartbeat travels with my voice along the airwaves. It's strong, radiating love towards you.

This program is for you, seeker of truths.

This program is for you, Universe's nomad, so that you can continue to intensify your inner glow.

This program is for your inner warrior. It's about time you opened the door so that she can come out to strengthen you and train your will.

This program is for those who are drowsy and want to speed-up their awakening.

This program is for those who have reached the top and want to keep climbing.

Don't judge people if you don't know them well, and when you think you know them, don't judge them either. What do you know about their lives, about their innumerable past lives?

Tell me what you're chasing after and I'll tell you who you are. Are you running inwards or outwards? Do you go after truth with the same intensity with which you go after superfluous, fashionable things? As you come to identify yourself with your Inner Wisdom, it's likely that abundance will come to you. They often go hand in hand.

Fashion and the media sell you an image of success and you accept it with your eyes closed. You think, "How can they be wrong with so much knowledge available to them?" And they reaffirm it: "Everything that's not on the winner's list is a guaranteed disaster and will put you in line with the losers". You keep nodding your head and mind, and are grateful for the list of everything you need to do, or have, so that you can be in the winners' photo.

They tell you that they're going to take you to the kingdom of wonders, and, since you like big meals, trips to exotic places, luxury and comfort, you sign-up for it. You forget that your Love Energy dwells in your inner landscape. Maybe someday when you discover that what they've sold you, which you recklessly chased after, doesn't stimulate your inner happiness, you'll decide to take a glance at your splendid landscape. It's your choice. I can only show you what's there. You're the one who chooses which direction you take.

What complicates your life a lot is planning something to the last detail, and if it doesn't turn out as you wanted, that puts you in a bad mood. The more carefully you've planned something, the more likely some things will go wrong, and you'll handle it badly and categorize them as failures: "I'm unlucky." "Today's not my day." "I'm not very clever." "I'm so unfortunate"… You demand absolute perfection from yourself and from life, everything needs to turn out as you've planned, instead of allying yourself with moderation and balance.

What are you accomplishing with your perfect plans? Filling up your agenda. Why don't you leave empty spaces in your daily planner? So that Life can make the necessary adjustments and decisions. Don't oppress it, set it free. Life always knows what's best for your growth. Where is the adventure, surprise, amazement of the unknown in your journey? Look, your hurry to reach your goals will reduce the improvisation, the game in your life, the fascination of being with all of your senses in the present. Try thinking about using a less rigid daily timetable.

Look at that little boy in the park. He's chasing a ball and trips, falls, and starts to cry uncontrollably. He trips and falls a few more times, but doesn't cry anymore. At one point, he pretends to trip and intentionally falls to the ground! What's happened? He's discovered that falling can be amusing and fun, and he's decided to incorporate this into his game. It makes you think, doesn't it?

Watch how you behave, how you take a task and make it shorter, as short as possible to make it easier and so that it doesn't cause you any kind of problem. You want to finish it, get it out of the way as soon as possible, urgently, so that you can immediately get started on the next task... You don't get any enjoyment in doing it. Sometimes you want to finish so fast that you only eat the cherry on top of the cake and you throw away the cake... You're in such a hurry to reach the top that you miss the beautiful landscapes on your way up. What is your hurry? What impedes you from enjoying the world around you? Identify it, and tell it clearly that you don't like being rushed.

You don't enjoy your task because you've classified it as unrewarding, insignificant, that it isn't good enough for you and that it can't teach you anything new. You don't play with it. Why don't you make it a counter for your life's game, and instead of suffering have fun with it?

Go back to the park's playground, a little boy fills and empties his pail with sand infinite times, lost in thought, focused in his game, with all his senses devoted to his task. He's having fun alone, he doesn't need friends or an audience to watch and applaud his ego. He's happy with just his game and a friend that shares in his fun: Life. How much does he get paid for all of that work? Nothing. What does he get out of it? Delight. Enjoyment. Fascination. He gets paid in another kind of currency. The coins he receives are minted by the thrill of exploration, discovery, creativity, living… Entertaining himself and being good at what he's doing makes him very happy. Today he's exploring in the park. Tomorrow, he'll explore the stars.

The other day, I was in a coffee shop. A woman came in and, standing, ordered a coffee at the counter. She grabbed it from the waitress' hands and drank it in one gulp, leaving the money next to the cup and ran off, with her mouth on fire I imagine. Compare this with the slow tea ceremony, where the goal is to celebrate the dance of movements, flavors, aromas, people, Time, Life…

Your enemies are your fears, your attachment to things, your hurry. Up until now they've beaten you, but now they're in a bad state because you've woken up your inner warrior. She's set on winning: widening your consciousness, love, peace, detachment amongst other things.

It's a good idea to remember that all the material things that you're collecting like a little squirrel, you'll have to leave behind at customs when you move to another dimension. You'll only be able to take your backpack of stars. The best thing would be that from now on you dedicate more time to filling your luggage with light. It's in your hands, it depends on you, on your will, on how much time your inner warrior spends sleeping on a lounge chair.

Having "love stocks" has a lot of advantages. You can obtain them anywhere, under any circumstance, without recommendations or having to pay to take classes. Once you have them, they're yours forever. No matter what happens with the stock exchange, the value of your love stocks will always increase. They'll be with you during all of the stages of your existence. The lessons you need to get love stocks are in your heart and are taught by your Inner Master. You get into the class through meditation, focussing your mind's attention on your heart.

Today my pearls of wisdom have run for a long time. I've heard some yawns from those in the back rows. I hope I haven't bored you. Until tomorrow, friends. Light, love and peace".

Thank you, Singer, the sound of your simple and clear words are like the soothing sound of a natural spring. They don't bother or tire me. They lull me.

I'm getting used to enjoying the fragrance of the ideas bouquet that books offer me. Their music excites and intensifies the dance of my emotions.

Book, you're a good friend. Your serenade of feelings rocks me back and forth, caressing and reconciling me with life. Book, dear book, thank you for always being ready to receive me, with your open, loving words, consoling me in my times of confusion and sadness. I know that I'll always be able to count on your bright voice to show me the way...

I've got messages. I'm positive that they're from the group. They just don't want to accept that my decision to stop going out with them is definite.

"Hey, cave girl. Today's your lucky day. You're invited to a party next Sunday at ten. It's going to be a late one. Put it on your list of essentials. Bring your sadness, it'll balance out our madness. Don't forget to bring drinks and something to munch. Bye cave girl, and stop frowning..."

Very funny and witty opening, and that thing about the list of essentials. Essential for whom? For you or for me? Don't pass your dull problems on to me. They're yours, you deal with them.

You have the same light as me, and I'm fond of you, but now it's time for me to move up on my own.

I have to draw up a plan to get rid of the loneliness I feel. Relying on the group didn't do the trick. On the contrary, it exacerbated the situation. I've got to work on it with my own effort, feeling better while I'm at home, not running away every time I feel alone, trying to block it out with the street racket. I'll use some other methods. I'll accept my sadness by thinking that its doing me good: "I thank you, sadness, because you make me more patient, tolerant, humble, stronger, more human and silent." And after awhile I'll take it, stick a stamp on it and send it off to infinity. And every time it comes back, I'll play the game again: welcoming it, accepting it and sending it off until it gets tired of coming back.

Little by little, it'll start disappearing. I don't have to learn by suffering anymore, but with luck, will, organization, enjoyment... Before, my complexes made me chase after everyone else to convince them... to convince myself of my worth. I looked for their approval in their applause, their admiration, their fondness, because I wasn't sure about my self-worth. Now, that's not necessary. I recognize the beautiful being I've always been. I shake it so that it wakes up. It's difficult for it, but I'm getting good results.

The Gift

It's pleasurable to watch the sunrise, the majestic way it move in slow motion. It's telling me, "Eva, do as I do. Don't stumble through your day. Dance with Time, without pushing it, without abusing it, without getting angry with it because of his rhythm. Go forward as I do, smoothly, radiating harmony, love, peace and light to everything and everyone. Accept the night with the same attitude, without regret. Your days, your time, is infinite."

At last, the big day has arrived! Delivering the book to Ric. Once again, my pockets are empty, but I'm up to date with my payments. I don't owe a single coin. Renting out the parking space, leaving the car and the group has made eating everyday possible.

I've missed Ric. I hope he makes it to our meeting. I'm impatient. Nervous. What if he doesn't show up? Maybe he could have forgotten the date, maybe the publisher could have backed out, maybe he's sick... A thousand things could have happened. Maybe, maybe, maybe... Wow, I'm so negative! Enough already with so many "maybes"! Hypothetical thoughts don't bother me anymore with your omens. I practice positive affirmations frequently, but I still don't know how to stop my negative thoughts. Every time I feel that they're bothering me, just seeing how they come close to my mind, trying to enter, I'll grab my new digital broom and beat them until they leave, running at the speed of light, rushing off, terrified, not knowing what is hitting them.

I don't let them waste my neurons on their favorite egocentric little battles anymore. I don't let them soak me with their scary downpours either. With my improved mental strength, I don't put up with them for even a second. I immediately substitute them for useful thoughts, full of strength, optimism and truth.

Okay, I'll be consistent and think positively immediately: Ric has come to the meeting, he's already waiting for me. He'll greet me with his warm smile and we'll share a deep hug. That's how it will be.

Yes, yes! He's sitting in the same place as last time. He's seen me. He smiles. He's coming toward me. We hug. A long, warm, emotional hug. What a moment! I'm floating.

"Welcome, Eva."

"It's so nice to see you, Ric. I really wanted to see you."

He steps away, and he looks at me smiling for a long time. His glance moves to the book.

"You did it! Congratulations. Come, let's sit down. Wow, such attractive presentation! It looks like a published book. You've surpassed yourself, you can see the care you've put into its creation. You've even made a cover. It looks great. A butterfly flying through a star-filled sky. It's very nice. Did you design it yourself?"

"Yes. I took photos of mountains, clouds, waves and butterflies with my digital camera, downloaded them on to my computer, and then I made a collage with them, combining them to create one image, and applied some artistic filters to it. It was fun and creative."

"I like the size and font of the letters. They are easy to read. That'll be good for people who have sight problems."

"Here's a CD with the text and the cover, in case you need to make copies."

"Yes, that's a good idea. If the original is lost, it's essential to have it."

"I liked your story a lot. I was expecting an academic text full of references with names and numbers. You've nailed the right tone by getting the reader closer to what insects feel, their circumstances, vicissitudes, what motivates them to act: surviving, defending their territory, reproducing, their daily battle for food…

You've gotten close to their emotions: fear, anger, pain... You put emphasis on the life force that beats inside of them. You've pulled off an entertaining narrative, graceful, that surprises, moves and hooks the reader with the power of a novel.

I've learned a lot from your book, Ric. I've come to look at insects in a different way. Before, I hadn't thought about the many extraordinary qualities they possess: their intelligence, talent, skill, bravery, will, perseverance...

It surprised me that there are so many kinds of butterflies. I didn't know that a lot of them are disappearing. Maybe it's because of the rise of global warming, which has been sharply increasing in recent times. Action needs to be taken now because it's getting worse.

You describe with a lot of feeling and strength the Monarch butterflies' wonderful migration, an epic voyage of approximately four thousand kilometers, full of happenings. It's an admirable feat for these fragile creatures to cross a whole continent. Many of them will die from exhaustion or from the dangers of such a long journey, in an endless battle against the heat, wind, rain, fatigue and predators. You make a song out of their odyssey, their bravery and enduring will."

He's such a good listener. He is pleasantly attentive to what I say without interrupting me or showing impatience even though I'm going on and on.

"Ric, I love how the caterpillar turns into a beautiful butterfly! It reminds me of the story of the frog that turned into a prince. I'm fascinated by how it instinctively makes a cocoon and comes out of it transformed into a graceful butterfly, flying instead of dragging itself. It's a hopeful message for those of us that aren't content with ourselves: there's always the possibility to change, as hard as it may seem, you don't have to give up. A moment will come when we'll be surprised to see how our wings spread and we can fly off."

"That's right, Eva. If a caterpillar can create its magical cocoon and come out with wings and fly away, imagine what people could accomplish with the power Life has put inside of us."

"How do I make my cocoon, Ric?"

"You already have it within you. Life has put it inside of you. It has always been there. Your butterfly is waiting for you to lower yourself down to your heart and open its nest. It's ready to leave, to try out its wings and practice flying with them. Through meditation practice you'll liberate it and the winged angel that you are will emerge."

"Your words have touched me. They make me want to put more effort into my feeble mental quieting exercises."

"You'll get there eventually. The trick is to keep at it. It doesn't matter if you throw in the towel every now and then, we all have ups and downs. What's important is that you pick it up again, as many times as you throw it in. A tree doesn't grow in a day. All the creativity and diversity that surrounds us has perfected itself over millions of years."

"You know what, Ric, I usually see things in a superficial way. Whatever is marvelous is reduced to being normal, and it goes unnoticed by me."

"That's the way it is, Eva. We tend to wrap up our senses, feelings and emotions with our personal issues, selfish interests and unimportant stories. With them, we construct a little fort with tiny windows that shrink the beautiful landscape and make it difficult for us to appreciate that we're surrounded by miracles. And to make our vision even worse, we devote ourselves to choosing a profession, career or job in terms of how much prestige, money, fame or power it will give us, instead of by how much joy and fulfillment in doing it will bring us during the course of our lives."

"Ric, my loneliness, my sadness are my forts."

"They're helping you grow. Soon, they'll leave you."

"How do you know?"

"I know."

That's the same answer the daisy seller gave me!

"Happy birthday, Eva."

"You remembered! Thank you, Ric."

"I have a gift that's going to surprise you. I think you'll like it."

"What a nice touch! Should I close my eyes?"

"Yes, imagine a marvelous shelter in the middle of nature, in a dream-like valley, surrounded by fabulous landscapes. Well then, as well as being paid for the translation, you'll get an all expenses   paid vacation to that paradise. Don't be surprised. It's compensation for delaying what I owe you, which is due to financial reasons. You can stay in that paradise until I pay you the total amount. You'll receive food supplies and everything else you'll need once a week. You don't have to take money, as you won't have anywhere to spend it. Once a month I'll deposit money directly into your bank account to cover your fixed expenses, so that you can enjoy the vacation without any worries. You'll get the deposit receipt along with your weekly supply. I can take you to the shelter in my car."

"Don't say anything else, Ric. I accept, I accept. I've wanted to get in touch with nature for some time now."

"I'm glad that you're excited about staying in the valley."

"Yes, I've had a very clear impulsive acceptance. Look, you can keep the book so that you can arrange the publication."

"I haven't paid you yet. Keep it until you get paid in full."

"I trust you, Ric."

"Thank you, Eva. It's a very nice touch."

"When can you take me?"

"Starting now, whenever you want. My car is parked at the corner."

"Great, I'll go home and get my bag. I'll be back in a couple hours."

"Perfect, so I'll be back in the middle of the afternoon in time to go to an interview. Don't overpack, in the shelter you'll find everything that you'll need. If you're missing anything you can ask for it and it'll come with the supplies."

"Well, see you in a bit, Ric. I'm eager to get to that paradise."

"Okay, Eva. I'll wait for you here."

At first, I was upset by the payment delay. Then, I saw the benefits that the change brought. I came out winning the vacation that I've wanted for so long and he's also going to deposit money into my account every month. I know I'm going to get paid for the rest of the translation. Deep inside, I trust Ric.

I can't believe it. Who could have known this morning that today I was going to start the vacation I've been desiring for centuries? I'll be able to breathe fresh air in the middle of nature and also have all the expenses paid for.

Ah, Singer, you've already begun. I'll listen to your appeasing voice while I pack…

"Do you know why you don't like to lower your mind to the splendid paradise that resides within your heart? Because you aren't interested, you need to have the same interest that you have when you're watching your team play. Because you aren't conscious of the immense richness and joy that confines it. Because you think it's boring and complicated. Because you lack interest and you don't practice it enough. Because you ignore its exquisite flavor and see it as an obligation. Look at it as if it were a game. Its rules are simple: you play while comfortably seated, without having to move, just like you would watch a TV program, with the benefit that you can watch it with your eyes closed, because the screen is inside of your heart. "How many players are there?" Two, your Inner Wisdom and you, but they don't compete because they play on the same team. "And how do I play?" Easy, you lower your mind to your heart through meditation. "And what's meditation?" I'll explain it to you. Meditation is giving a "good sweeping" to the thoughts in your mind, leaving it quiet, clean, empty of ideas.

Once it's empty, you lower it to your heart. "And how do I give it a good sweeping?" Easy. You sit down comfortably, close your eyes, relax, focusing all of your attention on your breathing, how air goes in and out of your lungs, that will keep thoughts out of your mind. Now you've got it calm and empty, ready to lower down to your heart, you'll do so by directing your attention to it.

Okay, now you're in your heart's box seat, paying the same attention as you do when you're watching your favorite show. Listen, feel, get emotional, applaud and give standing ovations to your soul's states… in silence. Make this your favorite challenge. You'll find your best holidays traveling along your internal routes. Do this every day, even if only for a few minutes, so that you don't forget it in your trunk of old memories.

"I lower my mind to my heart." It's the diamond on your bright necklace. You won't find a program like this one, no matter how hard you look. If you watch it everyday, putting all your interest into it, you'll become a being full of light, love and peace. All you need to do is plug your mind into your heart. "I lower my mind to my heart." I'm receiving your question: "How long will it take me?" You can guess what I'm going to say in reply: "It depends on how much interest you put into it."

I think that today you're more receptive. I'm going to give you some more bright lights.

Life is a dance. What are you waiting for? A partner? You're your own partner. You have it inside of you. Discover it now. Enjoy your dance with your partner. You dance for the Universe and the Universe dances for you. It's your partner. What else do you need? When you join your steps to Its moves, you become magical, a pure shaft of Light.

Life gives you signs, opens windows that offer you opportunities to change what you need and, sometimes, you don't see them or you label them incorrectly. You think they're bad luck, disgraceful, a punishment… instead of seeing them as a starting flag to begin the race toward something new that'll strengthen your wings.

Why don't you take out your warrior, your inner strength? What are you waiting for to shake off her dust and use her for the first time, transforming her from the doormat that everyone steps on, into your flying carpet? She's been waiting for such a long time for you to make up your mind and you're still dazed. She longs for you to free her so that she can fight for your qualities using her favorite weapons: compassion, tolerance, humility, bravery, strength, love... She can change your flashlight into a lighthouse. You decide.

A lot of people send peace from their hearts to the people and places around the world that need it. Dedicate some time, if you feel like it, to closing your eyes and lowering your mind, quiet and peaceful, to your heart, and from it, add your heartbeats filled with light, love and peace to theirs.

If you want to find the answers to your questions, look for them in your heart's silence. It has all of them.

You can imitate the behavior of children playing games. They don't do it for medals. They still haven't installed the brakes: "What will they say about me?" "I do it better," "They're going to laugh at me," "I'm going to mess it up," "I'm wasting my time," "I can fall and hurt myself," "What do I get out of this?"...

Sign-up for life's flow, for what you feel. Be true to yourself, without realizing you're acting as a mirror for others. Your ways, your attitudes reach, awaken and orientate those that surround you.

Today is your lucky day. Be aware of the great privilege of being alive during this special time in the world. Live it. Don't miss out on anything. It's your time, your chance. Clean the plate. Enjoy every last crumb. It's a good time to spread yourself out. What was closed before is now opening. You have a lot of resources at your disposal with which to find out truths: books, magazines, TV, Internet, radio, courses... Look for the best of the best and use them.

From now on, leave behind moldy pasts and uncertain futures. Don't give them your power, wasting your precious time thinking about them. Enjoy your life's movie in the present.

There are people who are immensely happy and have nothing. There are people who have everything and have unhappy faces.

There are many hearts, like yours, that want the world to be a better place, without poverty, war, injustices... The change begins with you. Be the way you want the world to be. Fill yourself with love, peace and light. Spread them, be generous, transform yourself into a lighthouse.

You are complete. You have everything inside of you. It's just a matter of finding the diamond that you are and picking off the layers of slag that cover it, making it shinier each time.

Think, speak, act impeccably. Dedicate some time everyday to practice meditation and, most importantly, feel love for yourself, for others, for everything, for the Universe.

Live the phases that Life puts you through with happiness and fullness. When one ends, let it go, don't attach yourself to it. Concentrate on the next one."

"I've got to leave you, Singer. I don't want to keep Ric waiting. Thank you for your wise and loving suggestions. They're helping me a lot. You're great. I love you."

The Four-Leaf Clover

"Wow, Ric, what a great four-by-four!"

"It's safe and comfortable. If you want, you can recline the seat and it will help you to relax."

"Yes, that would be good. I tend to fall asleep during car trips and I went to bed late last night. I was celebrating with some friends."

"Eva, wake up. We're here."

Whose voice is that? Where am I? It's hard for me to open my eyes. Oh! It's Ric. I've been asleep the whole trip. Have we arrived? Where are we?

He opens the door so that I can get out, it's a nice touch. One of my feet has fallen asleep. Oh! What a beautiful place! There are so many flowers with intense fragrances, the combination of their scents is strong. The air is so clean. There's so much light. The sun is drowning everything in a cascade of light, brightening up the colors of everything it touches. Wow, there are so many yellow daisies, my favorite flower. What a coincidence! I've seen them so many times during my life, but never so many in one place. This valley is incredible. Trees with exotic orange flowers. Those over there are covered in tiny clear blue-violet flowers. As the wind blows, they fall like snow.

No horns, no radios blaring, no washing machines running... What a festive, jubilant, joyful place! It's a carnival of light and movement. What spectacular havoc the birds have organized, with their busy flights, each one going their own way! They vibrate, moving the air with their comings and goings. They've got a good party here with the revelry of their humming. The butterflies add to the fun too, dancing with the flowers. The leaves aren't left behind either, fluttering and fanning each other, floating with the breeze's help. The flowers tremble excited by the wind. The tree's branches split the sun's light into an infinite amount of rays that dance to the rhythm of its leaves.

It's a paradise where everything breathes life, inviting me to join the game of Life. Wow, there are parrots! They're so loud, they sound like an orchestra of saws. What bright and striking colors they have! They're color in movement. Everything breathes with the desire to live. This little valley is like a circus full of miracles. Being surrounded by mountains gives it the intimacy of an interior yard. It's charming and strong, an eleven-star place. A magical, dazzling, paradise. It has good energy.

"You're thrilled, Eva. I can see you like it."

"Yes, I love it. It's like something from a dream, Ric. It's made me forget about the shelter. Where is it? I'm anxious to see it."

"There, behind the daisies and beyond the trees."

"I only see a rocky wall, covered in a tangle of vines and bushes."

"The shelter is right there."

"I don't understand anything. It's a rocky area, without any sign of the shelter."

"The architect who designed the shelter was a big fan of nature, he worked very hard to incorporate it into its surroundings so as not to lose the location's charm. He came up with the idea to take advantage of an existing cave, excavating it until he had a space that was habitable, functional and comfortable. He achieved the perfect harmony between the shelter and nature. The outer appearance doesn't reflect the inner spaces, which are warm, comfortable and cozy."

"He succeeded, so much that you can't see the shelter at all. It's invisible. The shelter is a cave… I think that architect was a little crazy. What an extravagant idea to build a shelter inside a cave!"

"When you see the inside and get to know its features, I think you'll change your mind."

I'm not amused at all. I thought I would find a rustic, log shelter.

"They call the shelter The Clover because if you look at it from above it looks like a four-leaf clover, the lucky clover. The architect was well-known for his project's originality and his innovative use of materials. He loved very much his vocation."

I love the place. It's strikingly beautiful, but I'm dazed, confused, depressed… The shelter is a remodeled cave and I'm allergic to closed spaces. I'm starting to think this situation is unusual, strange. I don't understand anything. Maybe Ric is joking and this shelter doesn't even exist, that it's all part of some joke at my expense. I was hoping to find a mountain cabin with walls made out of stone or wood, with a slate roof. No one would say that inside those rocks there's a shelter. I don't think I'm going to stay, I've suddenly lost enthusiasm. It's gone right to the ground.

I can't stand closed spaces, I wouldn't be able to live in a cave. It could be wet, have leaks or even bats. I'm not going to stay. I'm definitely going back to the city. I don't even need to see the shelter anymore. I don't want to live in a hollow cave, barren and icy. What a disappointment because I really like this splendid place, it's wonderful! I dislike the idea of going back to the city, missing out on all of this. In the city I don't have any money. I'll lose out on some paid holidays. He said it was a comfortable shelter surrounded by trees and mountains and the only thing he was right about were the trees and the mountains.

"Is something wrong, Eva? You look sad."

"Yes… I'm a little disappointed… I've got a feeling that I'm not going to like the shelter. I don't feel well in gloomy, closed places without windows, like grottoes, caves, caverns or whatever you want to call them."

"It's got very wide windows and a fantastic skylight in the bedroom. Come, the best thing is to take a look and judge for yourself. It's difficult to get an idea without seeing the inside. You'll be surprised."

"Yes, that's what I'm afraid of."

"Let's get closer. Appearances and imagination can sometimes trick your mind."

"I don't see the windows or the door anywhere, Ric."

"They're made out of a very resistant material that imitates the rock's texture. Its joints are identical to its seams and surface color. When you're inside, you'll be able to distinguish them."

"Where's the key hole?"

"It's a kind of lock that doesn't need a key. It works with a password, a code."

I think he's making this up.

"I'll show you how to open it. Stand right here. That's it. Place the palm of your right hand on the rock, just above this drawing that looks like a sun. Don't move for a few seconds. Good, the door's sensors are registering your energy's code."

I refuse to continue with this charade. I feel ridiculous and very sick. He's disappointing me. I trusted him so much. I hate it that he's trying to deceive me, that he's mocking me. I have to try very hard to hold back my tears. It's my fault for putting him on a pedestal. I don't understand his behavior. He's either been drinking or had too much sun. I don't understand why he's playing this joke on me, I don't find it funny at all. A few moments have passed already, so it must have my code, or whatever it's called, and the door hasn't opened. Just as I thought.

"Very good, that's it. From now on, every time you put your hand on the circle, it'll open."

Great, the moment of truth has arrived.

"I'm going to try opening it."

"Wait. Contain your impatience for just another moment. It would be useful if the sensors could recognize your voice as well, so that you can open the door with a phrase."

This it too much! I was afraid of this! He doesn't know how to end the game so he's prolonging this tragic play. I'm sick of this,

I'm going to tell him that I refuse to go along with this infantile comedy.

"That's okay, it's not necessary. Opening by touch is enough."

"The voice-recognizer is an interesting feature. It might be important in case you need it at some point. Please, Eva, it'll only take as long as it takes you to say the phrase."

"Okay, and then we'll open the door. It'll open without any further ado?"

"Consider it done, without any further ado."

"What phrase? I can't think of anything. Can you help me? I'm really nervous."

"Of course. "I'm Eva Luz." What do you think?"

"Yes, I like it a lot, it's beautiful, Eva Luz... it sounds familiar. Why are you smiling, Ric?"

"Because you're wonderful, Eva. You're looking at me with your mind's eyes, instead of looking at me with your heart's eyes. Can you see me from your heart? Do you want to? Do you think I could deceive you, Eva? That I could make fun of you?"

"No, I don't think so... It upset me to think that the shelter didn't exist, that I would have to go back to the city... Sorry, Ric, I feel bad for not trusting you, for losing faith in you so easily, that my trust in you has been so weak. I was disappointed, discouraged, confused because I didn't see the wooden cabin that I thought I would find."

"Don't feel bad, your reaction is understandable, forget about it. You were disappointed because you couldn't see a traditional shelter. It's my fault for making you deal with such an unusual situation."

He knows how to make me feel good about myself and not feel depressed.

"Thank you, Ric, for understanding."

"Thank you, Eva. And now, without further ado, can you say the password."

"Okay, here I go. I, I... I'm so nervous, I made a mistake, I'll try again. I'm Eva Luz. Yes, yeees, yes, hooray, hoorayyy, it has opened."

"You can go in, Eva. Welcome. This is your home."

Wow! It's beautiful, so bright! The material used for the windows that Ric mentioned is unique! It looks like glass, but from outside you can't see them. They camouflage themselves with the rock's surface. They're very wide, transparent, it's like being outside, among the trees. It's so spacious. What clarity! A pot with yellow daisies on the table! What a special touch! My favorite flower, and a tray with fruit. It's like being welcomed at a five-star hotel. The roof is dome-shaped, like an observatory. The light is so different and there aren't any lamps. It comes from the phosphorescent walls! It's such a welcoming space. And I imagined it with leaks. There's barely any furniture, only a table, two chairs and an armchair. It reminds me of my apartment's emptiness but it feels so warm! Okay, I'm staying. This shelter is extraordinary.

"There's the screen where you can write the list of food and things you might need."

"Where is it? I can't see it."

"It's on the wall. It's difficult to see, almost the same color as the wall. Let's activate it. You'll be able to see it better that way. The voice command to open the screen is: open screen, and to close it, close screen."

"Okay, I'll test it out. Open screen. Wow, it works! It's so easy to use. It's so big! It has a soft brightness to it."

"You can dictate to it, without using a keyboard or microphone. It has a speech recognition program that reproduces everything you say into text, immediately after you say something it will appear on the screen.

"Are there any limits to technological advance, Ric?"

"They don't exist. The Universe is constantly changing. It evolves with the creations of its creations. Nothing is permanent."

"That's so nostalgic."

"Nostalgia disappears if you stop looking at past achievements and you pay close attention to the bright and passionate surprises that life continually brings to you. Everything has been useful, it has all helped you to arrive at this moment. The creativity, progress and achievements of your ancestors are in you. Nothing is lost. Everything is recorded in the Universe's infinite memory."

"Ric, you said there were four rooms. Where are the other three?"

"Its doors are inserted so well in the walls that it's difficult to see where they are. You can open them by means of a voice command. Here you have some instructions on how to use the shelter with the most common commands. You'll discover them on your own. It will be a lot more fun than me showing them to you. They work with the same voice identification system that the front door uses. It's very simple. All you have to say is: open kitchen door, open bathroom door or open bedroom door. Try it out."

"Okay, let's see. "Open kitchen door". Wow! It really works! It's so fast and it opened the door really smoothly. I'm really starting to like this command system. What a wide window! It looks like there are tree branches in the kitchen. But it's empty! Is everything incorporated behind the panels aligned with the walls?"

"Yes, you have the commands and explanations in the shelter's instruction book. The shelter's features run on unlimited cosmic energy. All of its services are self-sustainable. They're all working. They haven't had any type of maintenance since the refuge was built.

This is like a shepherd's cane. It is made out of an alloy metal which makes it light and resistant. Always go out with it, it will be useful during your walks. Next to its handle it has this button. When you press it, it drives hostile animals away."

"Is it like a dog whistle that works with ultrasonic sounds?"

"Yes, that's a good comparison."

"You know what, Ric, I'm surprised by the shelter's design and resources."

"Yes, the civilization that its builders come from was very good at technological discoveries. However, the essential advances, those of the spirit and love, were left behind. Their arrogant desire for power divided them. Its inhabitants fought each other. They began to use their powerful weapons in wars. They didn't know how to stop. Their soulless technology became the weapon of their own destruction. They were exterminated, except for a few that were able to escape."

"Could our civilization end up the same way?"

"It depends if we can all wake-up the love and peace that we have within ourselves."

"It's a shame that their advances didn't help them in any way. We need to wise-up and not follow in their footsteps. We've still got time to fix our mistakes. Like you say Ric, if each person awakens peace within their heart and spreads it, peace on earth could be achieved."

"It's that simple Eva. I think your opinion about the shelter has changed. Have you decided if you'll stay or go?

"Yes, I've made a decision. I'm staying."

"If at any moment you decide to leave you can tell me through the screen, and I'll come and pick you up as soon as I can. It works like an email. You're not isolated."

"Thank you Ric, I'll keep that in mind."

"Well, although I do enjoy your company, I have an interview, and if I want to arrive on time I have to say goodbye now."

"I'll walk you to your car... Who are you, Ric?

"I'm a little light in this immeasurable Universe, traveling the path toward my return to the Light, just like you."

"What a great farewell!"

"You're the one who's great."

"You're impossible Ric, I like you a lot."

"Me too, our hearts are old friends."

"Can I give you a goodbye hug?"

"Of course Eva, we sing the same song. This beautiful valley will make you happy, it will erase your tears."

"You know about my tears?"

"Yes, it's important that you have strength during the first few days, so that you can handle being isolated. If you're able to stand it you'll receive prizes. All of your sorrow will disappear here. They won't follow you on your return to the city."

"That's wonderful news Ric, I've been yearning for that for a very long time. I'll resist. I won't give up."

"Enjoy everything that Life offers you in this valley. Look at this vacation as an example of how much it loves you."

"I'll live in the present. I'll happily welcome and unwrap all of the gifts that Life leaves at my door step. Don't worry, I'll be fine."

"I'm sure of that Eva, take care."

"You too Ric. Thanks for everything."

What a fantastic place! It's so magnetizing, so full of different aromas. Wow! I've never seen such beautiful butterflies! What a coincidence that there are so many daisies. I never get tired of looking at them, appreciating their beauty. I'll sit next to them in the lotus position and I'll fill myself with their breathtaking presence. I'm so lulled by the birds' singing.

What did Ric mean when he said our hearts are old friends? Was it only a phrase or did we know each other from another time? I've always found him very familiar... Well, I'll find out eventually.

I really love being on Mother Earth, filling myself with her harmonizing influence. The contrast between the white clouds and the blue sky is so intense. They move calmly. Contemplating them makes me feel a bit sleepy. With my eyes closed I can hear the sounds around me better. The sound that leaves make when they touch each other, pushed by the wind, reminds me of the sound that rain drops make when they fall on the ground. It's great being here. It's so peaceful it makes me feel sleepy...

I've fallen asleep! It's getting dark and it's cold. I'm going to put on a sweater…

I really want to know if the commands to open the bedroom and bathroom doors work. Where could the bedroom be? "Bedroom door open." There it is! It opens up silently. It's extraordinary! It's so wide, beautiful… Wow, the sky-light that Ric mentioned! The roof is arched and circular, too. Where could the bed be? Let me look at the command list…

I can't find it. Great! I'll have to sleep on the hard floor. Tomorrow, I'll be really tired. I'll try "bed out"… nothing… "Take out bed"… "Open bed"… Oh! When I stepped here the floor moved down a little, it's the bed! It's at the same level as the floor, I couldn't see it because it looks just like the floor. This is hilarious. I won't be able to fall off it. It's so wide! There aren't any sheets, with this summer-like interior temperature they aren't necessary. It's so enticing and so comfortable! It adapts itself to my body. It's placed directly under the skylight, it seems like I'm lying on a cloud surrounded by stars.

Gosh, I need to go to the bathroom now! It would be easy to go outside, pull down my pants, cover it with some earth and that's it… What about the toilet paper? Leaves? I'm going to stop thinking about possible solutions and I'm going to find the bathroom, most likely it will be extravagant. I'll check out how it works, it will be great fun… I guess.

"Bathroom door open." What's this? I don't get it, there are only bare walls. Where's the sink, the toilet, the shower? There are two traced feet on the floor here and among them a circle with some strainer-like holes. Everything is so clean. I feel bad doing it on this clean floor. I can't hold it in anymore… I feel better.

Wow! What a noisy vacuuming sound! It scared me to death. It's taken everything! What's this? A lukewarm water spout, and now a spurt of air, it's a small version of a hurricane, it almost lifted me off the floor!

Ric, you could have told me, I can hear you laughing from afar imagining my reaction to all of this. Everything is so clean and shiny like before and I'm totally dry. What a great invention! All of this is very strange for me. Maybe next time I'll do it outside, in the old-fashioned way.

This niche on the wall is probably the sink. I'll take a risk and put my hands in and let's see what happens… Maybe I'll do it some other time. It's probably broken, although, according to Ric, everything has been working well for centuries. I'm going to stop trying things out and I'm going to go outside and breathe some fresh air to see if I can get over this suffocating feeling I have.

I don't even want to think about it. If something were to happen to Ric I'd be lost. Only he knows where I am in this immense ocean of curled mountains. Go away negative thoughts! My mind, my imagination builds my reality. I need to learn how to control it, to stop it having negative thoughts that could harm me or ruin my day. I won't let my fears overwhelm me, worry my mind, disorientate it, taking away its desire and time to think positive thoughts. When my irritating and disturbing thoughts approach my mind they'll realize that they're not welcome, because my new generation flying digital broom will smack them so fast that they won't know what's hit them. I decide that I'm protected by Life and that's it, I forget about my fears. I'll only open up my mind to thoughts that make me more happy and noble, that make me grow…

Twinkling stars stand out in the night's intense blue. It's so beautiful, I've never seen them so close! The sky is very clear, I can see them really well. My concentration's sharpness has improved. I can control my mental noise more easily. I can focus my attention more perceptively and for longer than before, which lets me observe things deeply. Really, I'm using my eyes and ears for the first time.

Who would have thought this morning that I'd be in a valley looking at stars by nightfall?

I can feel my sorrows around me, trying to rain on my parade. In the city I'd avoid their solitude and neglect by sitting in a bar's terrace and distracting my mind by looking at the different city characters.

I'm so isolated here, so alone… There's no one to listen, applaud, whistle, criticize or disagree with me. No one that knows that I exist. No one that looks at me with kindness, affection, love…

To quash my arrogant ego, all I need to do is look at the endless sky, a mirror that reflects my minuscule magnificence in space and time.

Could there be someone on that star looking at Earth right now? Could its inhabitants be very different from us? How much love would they have in their hearts? Would they be filled with love? Would they kill each other in wars like we do? This question saddens me. It shows how much humanity is lacking in spiritual development… The crickets' sound is making me sleepy. Everything is full of life. The whole Universe vibrates…

The Prodigies Multiply

I should have asked Ric if there were any dangerous animals in these mountains. There was probably a reason why he mentioned the shepherd's cane to keep dangerous animals away. It might be a wise thing to keep it close at all times.

The darkness has become intimidating. The euphoria that I had when I first arrived has vanished. I feel alone, abandoned and a bit depressed. I'm starting to feel really tired. I miss the city. I'm a city person, I feel out of place here. I miss people, the urban sounds. What was that noise? Could it be a dangerous animal hiding in the bushes? The night's sounds scare me, I can't identify them. I feel as if I was floating in a sea full of sharks, but I can't see them. I've seen too many wild animal documentaries. This silence is scaring me. It seems as though it's yelling at me: "I don't want you here outsider. You don't belong here, you don't understand me, you can't appreciate me."

I miss my chatterbox friends, the background noise of my neighbors fighting, their kids screaming, the TVs buzzing, even the porter's sarcasm, the young carpenter's banging... Everything that distracted me and left me without any time to reflect on my own problems.

My sorrows can destroy the magic that exists in this wonderful place. I can make them weaker if, instead of fighting against them, I recognize and accept them as teachers that come here to improve my sensitivity, patience, humility, strength... "Hello, welcome, sit down and have something to drink while I deal with my chores... Oh, are you leaving already? See you next time." I am sure that someday they'll stop calling at my door.

I miss my childhood very much, my grandma's company, her words of wisdom. I need to be realistic, accept the present, although sometimes it's difficult for me. I think that my path, as for all humans, should be walked alone. I'm a Universe pilgrim in an eternal adventure toward the Light.

The smart thing to do would be to learn how to feel good with life and myself. When I learn how to love myself, everyone and everything, the joy of being alive will substitute my sorrow.

I was hoping that all of my troubles, including my sadness, would have stayed in the city, but they've come with me. They don't care if they're in a palace with golden rooms or in a dirty brothel, as long as they're the center of attention.

Who would have thought that an ad in the newspaper, along with an anything but conventional man, would have brought me here? This whole story has acquired the characteristics of a science fiction movie. The prodigies multiply: an impossible camouflaged shelter, built a long time ago with implausible technology...

I'm cold. I'm going inside the shelter. Ric said that the nights' temperature goes below zero, which could cause a person without protection or good equipment to freeze to death. I'll take note of that.

It's so warm! The light is so pleasant. "Close door." I feel safe inside, comforted. "Zero sound." Goodbye to disturbing sounds, this silence is peaceful. This armchair is something else! It feels like I'm floating on a cloud!

In the city I'd hang-up the phone and... Oh no! With all of the excitement of the move I forgot to take my cell phone and as far as I can see there isn't a phone here. I'll check "telephone out". It hasn't come out anywhere... It's not on the list. I'm isolated! Where do I go? Who do I call? Who do I talk to? To myself, to my warrior, the Great Eva, who's in my inner golden landscapes. I hope she wakes up completely soon. Ric told me I could communicate with him by using the screen but could I do it with my friends...?

Being here has been a big change. The ambulance noise has been replaced by the lull of the crickets' song, and the non-stop urban chatter has become the sound of the blowing wind.

The loneliness I'm feeling grows because of how immense this place is, lost in a desert of mountains. I feel like an abandoned child, forgotten on a planet, on a small pebble of sand that floats in the enormity of space. However, I know that I'm not alone. My grandma is still with me, and so are my parents, my guides and so on. But I can't look them in the eyes, nor listen to their voices, nor feel the heat of their hands. If I had the talents of dimensional channeling today which I avoided when I was a child, maybe I would be able to contact them...

Okay... I'm coming back down to Earth, with all the excitement of the unknown I haven't eaten since I arrived. I'll look in that eccentric refrigerator. Let's see what I can find. It's not on the command list. "Where are you my pretty refrigerator?" All of the walls are flat. "Where are you?" Oh, I've found it! The command is easy. I'll say it normally and clearly, just in case the voice identification system gets confused and smacks me on the face with any gadget it finds around. Well, I'll give it a try, "Re... refri..." I've made a mistake... "Refrigerator open." Yes, it's come out! Yahoo!

Wow! This is a supermarket. It looks like a fruit shop, there's such a great variety of fruits and vegetables. Great, they're organic. They're all perfectly organized in shelves located comfortably within arm's reach. It's like a library. It's so cool. It has the same brightness that the walls have. It has all types of food. What a surprise! Organic quinoa and millet. This bread is telling me to eat it. Let's see the ingredients: whole wheat flour, mother yeast, sea salt and spring water. A bottle of honey! It's not as if they know what I like. What are these beautiful bottles? Its extra virgin olive oil from the first cold pressing, such a luxury! This is... yes, sea salt. This is a coffee substitute made out of cereal...

I'm glad there aren't any heavy foods. If I don't have them I won't eat them. I won't ingest so many toxins and I'll have lighter and quicker digestions. That way I'll have more energy. My diet wasn't bad before, but this one, from what I can see, will be better.

My new diet is simplifying my life. I've reduced a lot of food incompatibilities and said goodbye to the dishes that make my stomach turn, swell, have gas… The person who sends me the food is addicted to healthy eating. It coincides with my diet profile.

I've slept well, like a baby. It's hard to open my eyes. Where am I? I can hear birds singing. I'm in the shelter! What a wonderful day! There's so much light coming through the skylight. The birds' singing is a great alarm clock. They're full of life and happiness. It's an avalanche of cackles, chirp-chirps and trills. Every one is concentrating so much on their own song that they aren't distracted by the others' rhythms. They're grateful that they can celebrate a new day and they demonstrate it by singing, enjoying it, exploring it, flying free, living… They must ask themselves: "Who has allowed this outsider to come into our territory?"

When I was back in the city I went to sleep at this time, dragging myself to bed. When the alarm clock went off I would turn it off and, without the will and the strength to get up, I would turn around and go back to sleep. By mid-morning I would drag myself out of bed, half-asleep and wrecked because of the partying I did the night before. Here, I jump out of bed swiftly with all of my cells awake, with my mind, eyes and ears wide open so that I don't miss out on anything that's going on around, just as if I were another little bird.

"Windows open" It's so magnificent! What a rich palette of colors! The flowers' colors stand-out so much with the plants' green background. What time could it be? There's not a single clock in the shelter. Who cares? I have the whole day in front of me. Free. I'll guide myself with the sun's position.

I jump outside. This fresh air is so stimulating. The birds are being really noisy. When I was a child, my grandma used to call me her little songbird because I would get out of bed singing. I feel radiant. It's surprising how my state of mind has changed, I was feeling so bad last night, but now I feel fantastic.

The sun lights up the color of everything it touches and it increases my good mood. I'm so lucky to have the opportunity to enjoy this blue planet one more day. Today I'll continue using my palette's new colors with my emotional paintbrush. I'll dive into nature's organized chaos.

Even the last leaf welcomes me. Everything has noticed my presence. Even the smallest sunbeam, the tiniest blade of grass has accepted me. I'm now part of the valley family. I can sense their invitation, "Eva, welcome. Come on! Join the party."

I'll enjoy my tree friends, the creatures of the valley, my laugh, my song, my dance. I'll take you out for a walk, my adorable inner child. We'll take a stroll in the forest and maybe you'll see a fairy. When you were a child you used to be able to see them and speak to them.

Before heading out I'll meditate for awhile. It will relax my mind and its trail of peace and serenity will accompany me throughout the day, helping me perceive and enjoy more in depth everything that life puts in front of me.

I take great pleasure in my breathing. I put all of my attention in how the air goes in and out of my lungs. I don't push it, I don't force it, so that it's like a soft, loving dance. Inside my chest I feel a fullness which is invading me. As I absorb its energy, its prana, its magic… I'm lowering my mind to my heart…

I could stay here all day. This breeze is extraordinary! I'll reflect for awhile. My reflections clear things up for me. They give me knowledge, develop my consciousness, make my mind responsive… Okay, go ahead, wake up ideas:

I can't see electricity or wind, but I know that they're there. I can't see the prodigious strength nestled within me, but I know it's there, that it exists. It's so surprising! It gives life, vitality and intelligence to all of my cells. They work so that my extraordinary body functions. They know what their task is and they put all of their zeal into completing it. They fight to the death carrying out their mission, keeping me alive, ensuring that all of my organs work perfectly. They figure things out on their own so that they don't have to depend on me. What other choice do they have? I don't know how my pineal gland, vesicle or pancreas work or what their functions are.

The magical strength within me is in charge of activating all of my bodily systems. They're very complex processes, like digesting food and assimilating their nutrients, directing each one of them to the place where they're needed. Meanwhile I "collaborate" eating all types of food, without worrying about chewing well to reduce the enormous work and wasted energy that digestion entails for my poor body.

Little by little I'm gaining knowledge from nature, from my grandmother's books, from what happens to me and from my reflections and meditations. Thanks to these internal and external experiences I'm coming up with conclusions about everything and I'm getting closer to the truth. I'm in an endless process of confrontation, reorientation, retouches, adjustments, keeping those that are accurate and getting rid of the ones that are not.

And so, as I develop my awareness and learn to listen to my Inner Wisdom, I advance, each time a bit more sure of myself, with more certainties in my backpack of stars.

I'm going to look for my neighbors. I'll take the same road that Ric took when he left in his four-by-four. Here are the tyre trails. He went until the end of this path and turned right. What a pleasant country smell! This is nature in its wild state. It doesn't need gardeners. It's taken care of itself for millions of years.

He turned right here. That's impossible! The path ends in an open area surrounded by trees without any exit. Where did he get out? The tyre trails finish here. The only thing that I can think of is that propellers came out of the car and it flew like a helicopter. I'm shocked... another unsolved mystery. I'm confused.

These locations don't match up with the ones in my country. The exuberant nature, the gigantic trees full of exotic flowers, the great quantity of different types of birds, parrots, butterflies... Where am I? I have no idea. I fell asleep during the trip.

It looks like the end of the world. These mountains look like a jungle. Why am I here, Ric? Why have you brought me to this valley?

I'm starting to think that this whole trip is part of a bigger plan, which is head by Ric and, in the summit, controlling the operation, is the Universe. Okay, I'm going to continue to enjoy the script and this exceptional scene in the movie. With everything that's happening to me my skepticism is falling apart. From now on I'm going to use "perhaps", "it could be" and "I don't know" more often.

A Shooting Star!

It's getting dark and I'm shivering. The temperature really starts to drop at this time. I'll go inside.

I'll sit down in front of this immense window, it's almost like being outside, among the vegetation. I'll contemplate as the afternoon languishes, as the evening prepares the stars' bed. I'll want to get used to the night's sounds, to familiarize myself with them and stop fearing them. "Cancel zero sound". The effect is impressive. It's like being outside.

The sounds are immersed in a deep, thick, tangible silence. It penetrates through my pores. I feel so small… and yet so grand. I'm a universe within the Universe. One of its particles. As I progress, I increase my consciousness and I'll be closer to understanding Its infinity.

If I were to send a cosmic letter, my return address would be:

Eva. The Four-Leaf Clover Shelter. Mountain 5.785.453. Blue planet. Solar system 4.768. Galaxy 37.450. Of course, I would stick on a stamp so that the intergalactic mail service wouldn't return it to me. I get lost in this super space dance…

It has suddenly begun to rain. It's getting worse. What a downpour! What sadness! I'm suddenly so nostalgic… Maybe it's because of the rain or having written my cosmic address.

My mental states and emotions aren't uniform. They alternate: happiness, sadness, loneliness, and so many others, intermingle. I must let my emotions flow from inside, so that they can manifest themselves through my thoughts, words and actions, so that they don't stagnate and damage me.

I rebel against you, sorrows. I'm in the most beautiful place in the world and with your misfortune and loneliness you try to transform it into a prison.

I don't blame you, Life. I know that it's my short-sightedness, my blindness, which prevents me from reducing the torture of my afflictions. I know that the Light that you give us is the same as someone who's born in a royal cradle or in a shack. Why don't I appreciate myself if I'm a precious being? Why so much confusion? Why do you torment me so much, sorrows? I feel so painfully underestimated. I twist and turn my misfortunes more than a wheel. I stick to them, instead of putting them on the street.

Maybe, Life, you gave them to me so that my talkative mind and my chatterbox lips can learn how to be more silent, so that I can dedicate more time to enrich my inner dialogue and to feel well without depending so much on the external.

Why, Life, do you dress me in misfortune? Yes, okay, I'm the one who chooses my clothes. It's me who doesn't know how to manage the freedom that you give me. It's me who entangles the ball of yarn of my existence over the course of the eras, so inextricably that I'm incapable of untangling it. I grow impatient with myself, I leave it aside and I irritably blame you.

I know that there are reasons for my desolation that escape my mind in its current evolutionary level. I'm like a snail that climbs onto a television screen, protesting "I don't like to advance on this fine surface. I slide, and its flashing bothers me. I prefer rocks." It can't imagine what's behind the screen. It will have to wait light years for that. "Now I understand what the purpose of that smooth surface that I climbed on eons ago was for."

There are also so many screens that I don't understand and that I don't value.

Maybe the snail didn't really want to change its protective and heavy caravan for some flighty wings. Maybe he doesn't believe that it's possible or considers it indispensable, it's his armor and his wagon. Maybe he thinks that some light wings wouldn't protect him so much, or he hasn't even thought of it, he only climbs and eats. Sorry snail…

Maybe the way to change my sorrows for joy would be to love, accept, and live with them giving them less importance. Perhaps then, happy to be recognized, they would vanish. I don't know.

It's easy to say it, but doing it… Right now they're attacking me with a lot of strength, I can't stand them. I need to speak, communicate with someone, to get rid of my restlessness, the inner fury that oppresses me for not knowing how to forget them. I'll go out and I'll yell, throw them out with all of my strength to the rain, to the wind…

Rain that falls over me. Rain, listen, yes, this is for you, I'm shouting at you. I violently spit my sorrows so that you can dissolve them with your deluge. Strong wind that shakes me with strength, drive them far away from me. Take them away with my voice across the mountains. I want, I want, I want, I beg to hear someone's words, please, please… I would give my kingdom for a phrase, a glance, a hug, an "I love you."

Never-ending sorrow, you're realizing that the joy that I'm experiencing in this beautiful valley is making you lose ground, and you attack me with even more fury, stop bothering me, get away from me, and leave me alone. I'm fed up with you and I'm fed up with myself for not being able to find the exit to your complicated labyrinth. Okay, you've won. I'm going back to the city where you won't bother me with so much impulse, with so much insistence. Here you hurt me even more.

My words come out like a thunderstorm, hoarse, pushed by my inability to contain my sudden rage of sadness. I'm unjust. I launch the rage I have within my heart against Life. This unrestrainable repulse is, in fact, toward me.

Universe, I shout at you with all of my strength. I can't handle the deep sensation of lack of love that I feel anymore. It oppresses and torments me. I've put up with its attacks a lot. Why don't you get rid of it? Why don't you listen to my pleas? Enough already! Stop! It isn't helpful to me to think that it's still not the time to get rid of it, because it's helping me grow. I can't handle it anymore. It's stronger than me. In the city it was quieter. I give up. I'm going back to the city. Please, please, please, sadness, solitude, I beg you, leave me alone and stop drowning me with your tears. Don't hide the joy that this great valley makes me feel.

I don't want past events to ruin my life. I don't want tied knots that will lower my mood. I forgive myself and I forgive you, whoever you were. I'm wrapping you up with all of my love. I want to begin from zero, with enthusiasm and happiness, with the desire to live.

I know that I'm interconnected with everything, with everyone, that feeling alone is only an illusion, but I miss the children and the elderly people I used to take care of. I miss having someone with a twinkle of kindness in their eyes looking at me...

I'm soaked, shivering. I'm going inside. I don't want to get a cold. I don't have anyone to take care of me... I'm wrong, I take care of myself. I'm going to make myself some thyme tea. I'll put on some dry clothes. I've let it all out.

I need to reconsider, see the positive side of being in the valley, it's growing on me. At first glance, I think I'm not making any progress. However, the new type of lifestyle in this natural space is making me feel better. It's soothing me. My sorrows are gradually going away. Ric said that they would leave. I'll endure them with patience the rest of the time that I have to live with them. I'll keep on waiting...

I'm disconnecting myself from the worthless thoughts that used to bother me in the city. I'm more open, more perceptive to new ideas, new ways of living, recognizing the wonderful being that I am. I don't look at my bellybutton so much anymore. I've confronted my ego. Now it's weak, without the arrogance it used to have.

As I observe my behavior, what I think, say and do, I discover clues that tell me who I am, what I'm like, but not what's causing my sorrows.

I am discovering the beautiful being that I am, that I've always been. I can see that with the changes I make, some of my old habits are starting to disappear.

Once again, I've overcome my assiduous sorrows' bullying. This time they've come with a lot of force. I'm not returning to the city. I've changed my mind. I'm here as Life's guest. I know that it's a great privilege. I'll stay. It has stopped raining, it's clearing up. What abrupt changes! The temperature outside is almost below zero. It's so comforting in this warm environment, through the protective window, to observe how the blue color of the sky loses intensity, getting closer to the mountains' gray shade. The clarity that bordered its peaks has disappeared. The mountains' gray color is gradually blending in with the sky's blue-gray, until you can't tell the difference between where one ends and where the other one starts. The mountain has flown up to the sky. Sky and mountain have become one. The stars are beginning to glow.

This is another world. It's so different to the city's noise, they have nothing to do with each other, honking, ambulance sirens, the upstairs neighbor's heels, television and chatter. They used to bother me but now I realize that they also kept me company.

This environment takes away what's routine. It opens me up to a purer mental state more adequate to receive the essential things: the personal secrets of my Ego, the Superior One, the same one as always, so ignored in the city by my old, hasty ways.

What a splendid sight! An applause for the shelter's architect. He put the bed exactly under the skylight. It's wonderful, made out of a single piece, without a single joint. It's like sleeping among stars... being another star... "Light two." What relaxing dimness. I've gotten used to the command system.

I feel so insignificant, so tiny, in this ocean of mountains, stars, galaxies. Wow! A shooting star, quick, a wish. "Take away my sorrows, I've cried enough. I want to be happy. I want to be light. I want to be Eva Luz." All of a sudden it came out, the name that Ric gave me when I opened the door! Wow! It's the same name my grandma gave me in my dreams, which I couldn't remember. My goodness! I'm going from one surprise to the next. It seems like Ric and my grandma are playing on the same team. Everything is so surprising.

Who's giving me the energy to continue navigating in a space and a time with no beginning or end? What keeps my inner warrior standing, feeding its desire to keep on riding, after having fought so many battles, life after life? Perhaps it's my bird friend, my sun friend, my butterfly friend, my elderly friends that I take care of and my babysitting friends. Perhaps it is because I want to continue to fill my backpack of stars with lights. Perhaps it is the curiosity of discovering this chapter in the novel of my existence. Perhaps it is the pleasure that I get when watching nature's show, or discovering truths, the meaning of life, or being a Universe explorer that walks toward the Light...

My eyes are half-opened. Sleep is beating me. I'll conclude my ideas about these issues. I'll continue my search to find the answers in another moment. There will be more occasions to do this. I'm eternal. What a hard day! I'll fall asleep giving thanks. "Thank You, Creator, for conserving my breath on this tiny piece of ground that floats in the infinity of time and space. Than... thanks grand... ma... take... care and take... care of... me...

The messenger

It's a good moment to give some pleasure to my sense of taste and my stomach. What am I going to have for breakfast? Something light, because I still have the energy from last night's dinner, plus the energy I have stored while I slept. I'll have a slice of bread with oil and some apples. They're delicious and they'll give me energy and won't weigh me down too much. That way my body will be light and my mind will be awake, feeling fresh during the entire morning…

With my grandma, before eating, we would thank the Creator for giving us food and blessing it. I had almost forgotten. I'll start to use it again. I also want to recommence the protection request that we used to say before going to bed and after getting up. We implored Him to keep our sphere of protective energy activated around our bodies, protecting us from everything that's not good, and also, to wrap our house and car with a sphere of protecting light…

What joy! Its great relaxing under the sun, feeling its warmth on my body. Something has landed on my leg! It's a butterfly! I'm going to move my index finger towards her slowly so I don't scare her. I'm moving nearer in slow motion, almost touching her. It's so strange that she doesn't fly away. I touch one of her small legs. It's incredible. She still doesn't fly away! She puts her legs on my finger and she climbs on it!

I just can't get over it! I'm moving my hand and she still stays on my finger. I bring her very close to my face so that I can look better at her extraordinary beauty. She's very brave. She continues to hold on tight to my finger, resisting the strong wind's push, which makes her wings flutter.

"Why have you landed on me? How did you know that I wanted you to climb on my finger? What did you feel? What made you trust me? Why don't you fear me? Why do you listen so attentively to me, as if you understood me?

Maybe you felt my love, the most beautiful energy, moving toward you, and to enjoy it you came over to me. "You came over to me." Those words comfort me so much, your visit, your company. You know what? Children are also sensitive to love. When a child is loved, as an adult he'll be a happy, noble and honest person, without traumas. Unhappiness, injustices, wars, hunger exist because of lack of love. Love unites and harmonizes.

My butterfly friend, except for my grandma and Ric, no one else has listened to me as attentively as you. Your attitude is moving me. Talking to you, sensing that you're looking at me, filling me with your esteem, your love, and knowing that you've stayed here with me, that you haven't left, is doing me a lot of good.

Now I understand the help a pet can give to a person with a lack of affection. It can be a good therapy for them. Love heals. It's a healer, the best medicine. Animals feel it and they share it generously, without asking for anything in return.

I'm moved by the trust that you have in me, that you're not afraid of me, even though my face may look gigantic to you. You know what, pretty butterfly? Your company, your uninterested and friendly attention is touching my sensitive side. Tears are rising directly from my heart.

Thank you for landing on me. Thank you for letting me speak to you. I greatly wanted to express myself, to communicate with someone. Thank you for listening to me with so much interest. Thank you for being my friend. Thank you for being so beautiful and filling my heart with your colors and feelings. Thank you for your simplicity. Thank you for your lesson of courage, responsiveness and detachment. Thank you for stoically enduring the wind's lash, without flying away, in spite of the huge effort it is for you. And thank you for being my mirror. You know, I love you.

I'm reconciling myself with a lot of things because of you. I know that you're a messenger. I'm sensing that you bring an invisible message to me: "Dear Eva, Life loves you. You're not alone, you're well accompanied. Everything spreads its love toward you."

You're consoling my heart's solitude. You're making up for that crisis that happened to me yesterday under the rain, and you're reaffirming my decision to stay in the valley. I admire you because even though I must seem a giant or a skyscraper to you, you stand here bravely, without fear. Your confidence, your instinct, your intelligence and your way of being are confusing me. In some places it's believed that when a butterfly lands on you, love has opened up in your heart. Oh no! I've made an abrupt movement with my arm, I've startled you and you've flown away. I feel so bad. You've left...

How beautiful and unusual it's all been... She's coming back! She's fluttering around me. I'm going to extend my arm with my hand facing up, like a landing strip. I'm naive. How can I think that she could understand that I'm holding out my hand so she can land on it?

She's coming down, getting closer to my hand. You've landed! You've landed! I can't believe it! You've understood me! Welcome, my dear and intelligent butterfly, you touch my soul so much. Your return makes me so happy. How astonishing! How complex! I don't know... or simpler yet... Love joins, and in this case it's joining two very different creatures that have something in common: we're both full of Love.

I'll meditate for awhile. I'll get one more glimmer to put inside my backpack of stars.

I'll remember, when I finish meditating, to come out of it gently, without getting up in a hurry, without making abrupt movements, going back to my normal state gradually.

I'm comfortably seated. I straighten out my back so that my chakras are aligned, and the energy that I receive from the Universe goes through it better. I relax my body. All of my muscles are loosened up. I close my eyes and silence my mind, emptying it of thoughts, focusing all of my attention on my breathing, peaceful, tranquil, without forcing it. I lower my mind to my heart... Each time I'm taking it to deeper, more peaceful states... My desires are dissolving. I don't need anything. I have everything... I Am...

Focusing my attention on my breathing makes me feel a gentle and pleasant warmth inside my chest. It's almost tangible, a feeling of fullness... It's a dance between the air and I, easy like a bird's glide, like the breeze. With each intake of breath, a welcome hug, with each outlet, a goodbye, like a soft tide. As I breathe, with my attention focused on it, my thoughts go away and my mind calms down, emptying, cleansing itself.

Breathing loosen me up, making me swift, lighter. It strengthens and pacifies my mind and spirit. It helps me get rid of my uncontrolled thoughts, concerns, fears... Its rhythm expands and contracts me, it gets me closer to the Universe's light, love and peace...

I can improve the exercise by imagining, visualizing that when inhaling, a ray of light from the Universe shines down on my head and travels through my spine until it reaches the solar plexus, from where it expands to all my body. It reaches all of my cells, covering them, filling them with its energy, purifying them, revitalizing them, filling them with health. When I exhale I visualize how the light flows outside of me. My intention is to share it, so I send it to people and places that need it, or I can let it choose the most appropriate destination.

I love to feed the birds. The bravest ones eat out of my hand, and some of them sit on my shoulders. I could have never imagined it! You're so small, so magical, you're the valley's singers. Your reason for being is singing, filling yourselves with joy and fulfillment with your songs and sending them in all directions, to whoever wants to receive your gift.

You're a good example for me, showing me how to celebrate the day. You start to sing full of happiness and you continue like this the entire day, recognizing Life. You separate, connect, pause and recapture the notes so well. I don't get tired of listening to you.

"How can you fly so quickly between the tree branches without crashing into them? Easy, you're not sleepy or absent-minded. You've practiced a lot and you're focused on what you're doing. Travelling light and living minute-by-minute, you are able to create your beautiful and risky acrobatics."

Here comes one of them. It's yellow and has something in its beak. It's left it on my head! Oh, what a nice gift! It's a small, yellow daisy. It reminds me of the golden gleam that the light being's dove put on my head during my dream! Thank you little bird, are you giving it to me or are you a messenger sent by the being in the dream, who was advising me to open myself up to the Universe's Strength?

A lot of strange things are happening to me. In the past I would have considered them incredible, unreal. Reality is intermingling itself with fantasy. I'm discovering the meaning of some of my dreams.

Thank you, Life, for your two gifts, which are stopping my impatience, my excessive hurries, and calming me down. The first gift was being in charge of translating the book about butterflies. It anchored me to the apartment, to silence, to solitude. It let me start practicing meditation and it strengthened my will not to succumb to the groups' invitations and other things that could have tempted me. The second gift, the shelter, The Four-Leaf Clover, is helping me to accept myself, to enhance my light, to listen carefully to my Inner Wisdom and to recognize the precious being I am.

I've never identified myself so much with the clouds as I do now. I'm so comfortable lying on the ground. It's so peaceful to feel the rise and fall of my chest as I breath.

A leaf. It's so weightless. It's so amazing how the wind blows it and it flutters around like a butterfly, getting closer to me. It has stopped in front of me!

"My dear leaf, I need to talk, communicate. There are times when I feel so alone. Do you want to listen to me? Do you want to have a conversation with me? You know what, I'm going to close my eyes and concentrate on your energy... Let's try it out... Let's see if it works...

My dear leaf, you're rising up, inward, trusting your heart's compass, revealing truths, ends without an end, ends that are a beginning, no trace of the past, with all engines blaring, going toward a new canvas. You've rid yourself of what distanced you from your beloved landscape: Your spinning-top ego. Your tight hands. Moneybox games, it's better to play with emotions. Glasses that deform reality, go away shortsightedness. Now you're ready to open your wings. Tell me, dear leaf, what are you looking for?"

"I want to swap the neon lights for my luminous inner landscapes and lose the records, diplomas, cards, empty achievements, delusion of grandeur. I want to feel the breeze and the sun, be part of the Universe... Be. I want to detach myself from mirages, nostalgias that hinder me, and from the things that I *have* to do but I don't feel like doing. I want to clear the dust from the open ticket and allow myself to travel toward my iridescent, internal landscape's magical symphonies."

"It could be, my dear leaf, that our conversation was a message from the being that has sent you to me. Or maybe it comes from inside of me. Your presence has made it possible and has made me receptive to it..."

A Road toward the Past

Okay, I'm about to start my first excursion. I have to be careful not to get lost. I'm going to jot things down in a lot of detail in my travel notebook, noting reference points along the journey, so that I'm able to find my way back. I'll mark it by tying ribbons on branches, so that I can always see the previous one. I can also, depending on the path, unwind some rope.

It looks like a square flagstone, carved by hand. It's about four spans wide. There's another one next to it, and another. It's an alignment. It looks like a tiled path covered with heaths, roots, moss, dead leaves…

The entire flagstone surface is engraved in a multitude of strange signs. I know what they mean! I've been here before! I've seen it several times in a past life. I don't know how I know it, but I know that it's true. This is so exciting and exhilarating. I feel the need to follow it. Let's see where it takes me. It goes into some dense vegetation that's going to be difficult to get through.

I'm wrecked. I've traveled a good distance. It's been a good walk. I'll stop for now and continue tomorrow. I've signaled the road so that I'll be able to return to this place as many times as I want. I'm starving, I'm going to have something to eat.

I'm going to name this place *Bridge toward the unknown* or *Path of the spirals and the suns*, although it wouldn't be bad to call it *Road toward the past*. It sounds mysterious and impacting. This enigmatic path fascinates me, encouraging me to continue. I'll keep on investigating it. I sense that I'm getting close to the end.

I'm going to forget about food. I feel an intense curiosity to know where it takes me.

I'm getting a vision!: "It's night time. I'm walking on this road, surrounded by many people who are carrying torches. We're all singing a monotonous song, like a psalmody"… It has been very short.

The leafy vegetation is opening up… Behind the bushes I can see an open area without trees.

What a great plain! With a monumental rock in the center. It's so mysterious… It's the same rock as the one in my dreams! They foresaw this event. So a plan exists. Who's writing it? Life. Who's Life's pencil? Ric? My disbelief continues to fall apart.

Its surface is covered with figures, signs and shape sculpted in bas-relief, traces of civilizations that have left their imprint here during the course of time.

Everything is so familiar to me. I'm going to go around the rock because I know that on the other side I'll find some holes that are used to climb to the top of the rock. There they are! It's giving me goose bumps. I've really been here during a past life. I'm not imagining things! The dreams I've had about the rock meant something. I'm living an event that has been pre-planned. My skepticism is falling apart like a house of cards. I'm afraid of going up, of opening my historical photo album and discovering things that I might not like.

How many civilizations could have met here over the passing of time? How many times could they have come together to speak with the stars, to invoke the Universe or to celebrate big events? I'm part of its history. I'm going to go up. I've got an impulse to climb it, but at the same time to get away from here. It's enormous, at least four times taller than me! Here I go… I'm so agile! I've gone up as fast as a squirrel. On the floor there's a sculpture executed in bas-relief with the shape and size of a real human body. I'm going to lie on it… My body fits it like a glove! The rock is so hot. The suffocating sun dazzled me. I close my eyes. I feel a vibration. Is it me or the rock that's vibrating? Or are we both vibrating at the same time? This is such a bizarre situation. A few months ago I would have considered it fictional.

The vibration is getting faster, I can barely stand it, and it's burning my chest. I'm going to stand up. It's hard for me to get up. It seems as if I am magnetized by the rock. Finally! Thank goodness for my boots, if not I would have burnt my feet.

The wind refreshes me, it shakes my clothes and it messes up my hair. It feels so great! I'm going to close my eyes to enjoy it even more. The vibration has eased. My chest is no longer burning. I feel so relaxed, it's so peaceful. I feel as light as an astronaut floating in space. This is a stellar, culminating moment.

What's happening? I'm going into a trance. I'm starting to get images from another time! They're constantly changing, coming and going, and overlapping each other very quickly, as if they were slides. I'm aware that I'm between two eras. I see a girl sobbing. It's me! I'm sure it's me in that life. A group of men dressed in long tunics are dragging her by force. She resists, she kicks and she lets herself fall. A great construction protected by a fortified wall. A group of children running cheerfully, covered by a cloud of dust. A woman in lotus posture with her eyes closed. Adobe shacks around the fortified wall. A big crowd walking disorderly, hastily. The image has fixed itself on a single slide: In the distance, there's a great rock with vertical sides. It's the same one I'm on, the one from my dreams. On the top, there's a woman. The image is getting closer. She's tall, thin, and she's wearing a long, indigo tunic, flapping in the wind. Her long, black, oiled hair almost reaches her waist. Dark skin. Deep, sad, black eyes. She seems to be absent-minded. Her gaze is lost in the distance. Her eyes see without seeing. Indifferent to what's around her. Everything about her gives off a great energy. I'm her! She's me! We're one. I can feel it. I know that I'm right. I recognize myself in her. I'm her during that era. I'm completely sure of that. I'm drawn to her. I'm in her body. Her body is my body, that of another time. I can see through her eyes. I have become one with her. My heartbeat is her heartbeat. My spirit in another life and in another body. Then is now and now is then. Time comes and goes. The present and past are now linked. They've become one. They've come together.

Somehow, I'm accessing the file where the events of that time are kept. I'm a spectator, but at the same time I'm part of the action. The border between what's real and fictional has disappeared. I'm living my reoccurring dream, where I saw myself standing on this rock.

Gusts of wind whirl my hair, violently shaking my clothes. I feel a skirt touching my legs, instead of my jeans. I'm afraid to open my eyes. Here I go. Wow, there are so many people! The raised area is entirely occupied by a great crowd! Why are they looking at me? What do they want from me? They're sitting on the ground, looking at me expectantly, fervently silent. The view has also changed. The bushes have disappeared and everything looks well cared for.

I have leaped in time. I'm occupying a body that's not my own. I'm wearing an indigo tunic. I'm dark-skinned. I have such beautiful bracelets. My fingers are long and slender and my fingernails are painted violet. My boots have been substituted by some leather sandals. My awareness, the perception of what surrounds me, is very alive, very awake. I know that I'm me, with one foot in this life and the other one in a past life. Both coexisting in the same unified time frame. My attention alternates between both times. There are moments when I'm only in one of them, forgetting about the duality that's occurring.

These two times in history become one because of Life's magic. Thank you for choosing me as the link.

Suddenly, strangely, the birds have stopped chirping. The strong wind has ceased. There's complete silence. I calm my mind and I lower it to my heart. My frequency rises. I can feel heat and energy within my chest.

I can sense an intelligent energy entering my mind. It's very loving and fills me with peace. It's familiar to me. I recognize it... It belongs to the master! The being of light that has been giving me messages for the community since I was a little girl.

I'm its voice. My mind translates the energy of his messages into the community's language. It flows effortlessly. Sometimes my personality can alter it, each time less. Time has perfected my talent in transmitting the communications that light beings give us.

My eyes close gently. I can feel a small smile appear on my lips. My face reflects peace and relaxation because of the love-energy that I'm receiving from the master.

"Welcome from the future to the recreation of the past. It will help you remember the mission you chose in another time."

"Master! Thank you for your welcome. I feel very happy to meet you again after so much time."

"Thank you, Eva, for returning, for continuing to be faithful to the task you chose."

I'm starting to receive his message. My words flow calmly, confident, full of love, peace and strength. Sometimes I pause with a sigh.

"Cover yourselves with humility and naturalness. Don't establish differences between those who wear sandals and those who go barefoot. Remember that greatness resides in the heart.

The path is inside of you. It goes towards the Light. We're all going in the same direction. The only difference is the place where we're at. The quantity of Light that everyone has received is the same. Some of them have been able to wake it up more than others. Some will arrive earlier, some later, but we'll all arrive.

During the day observe yourselves. Be aware of your thoughts, words and actions. That way you'll become more understanding, patient, wise…

Live minute-by-minute. Don't underestimate the here and now. Don't give your power to the future or the past. Live in the present.

Keep your mind quiet in your heart. It illuminates your path and guides your route.

You're too into the external. It's difficult for you to walk your mind through your inner gardens. Dedicate more time to keeping it silent so that you'll be able to manage your thoughts and have a peaceful, calmer mind.

It's difficult to control your mind in the chaotic time you're living in. You lose your attention because of your hurries, fears, interests, conflicts... Try to live within the silence of your heart more often, that's the way to preserve it.

Dedicate yourselves to getting rid of your old habits that stop your progress.

We adapt our teachings to your level so that you don't feel overwhelmed by a load greater than your strengths, and you don't get discouraged when you realize what a long road you have ahead of you. It's better that you focus on achieving your small goals. Looking at the summit from afar might dishearten you.

Don't let fears go into your mind. Flee from them as if they were the plague. They diminish your mental capacity, your strengths, and shorten your steps.

Raise your mind to high levels. That way you'll perceive the truth and love what Life sends you.

It's difficult to control a mind flooded with thoughts. Dedicate time to it, maintain quiet spaces for it, appease it and calm it down. If you persevere you'll gradually achieve it, getting ever closer to peaceful and fulfilling states, and every time you'll like going to your inner gardens even more.

Remember the importance of humor and happiness in your development.

Balance action with silence, dedicate time to contemplation, reflection and meditation.

Avoid vanity and arrogance. Keep a close eye on your ego. It's a talented manipulator, altering and distorting circumstances in its favor. Don't allow it to put itself on a pedestal, lifted up by self-praise.

Trust in your Inner Master. Lower your mind to your heart where you can find him, and learn to listen to him. Pay attention to his messages.

We show you the way and we encourage you to follow it. We don't do it for you because it would take your lessons away from you.

We return time and time again to the same topics because we know that with the daily noise that surrounds you it's easy to forget them. Sometimes we speak to you gently and other times we use more strength, full of desire that will motivate you even more.

Close your mind and lips to judgments. What do you know about people's lives that allows you to criticize them? Nothing when compared to everything they've lived during their many past lives.

Be Light and illuminate. Be peace and pacify. Be love and love.

Make your mind strong so that you can confront situations with peace, inner strength and without fearing any of life's experiences.

Throughout the day be attentive to your thoughts, words and actions. Try to have them emerge from your heart. They could be torches that will illuminate you, others and what surrounds you.

Don't think about your fears. Try to control your negative thoughts. Substitute them for useful, positive and luminous ones. Practice keeping your mind silent, quiet. It will provide you with very happy moments.

Light, love and peace."

The scene is fading... Once again my mind is blank... When the images of that time open up they go back and forth, like a slide show. Sometimes they overlap with those of my current life. Other times many images appear, compressed in a single slide...

The images from the past are returning, at normal speed. I see a little girl, about seven years old, who's sobbing. I'm her. My spirit is inside of her, in another time, in another body. Her thoughts come to me: I don't like this place. I don't want to be here forever. I'll escape. I don't like them. They're not nice. They're very serious. They don't know how to deal with children. They don't smile at me or say nice things to me. They only talk to me when they tell me what to do. They only like me because of my talent. I'm going to stop saying what I hear, but they won't let me do that. They'll force me. The days are very long, I get very bored. I can hear my friends making a lot of noise while they play in the courtyard. It makes me so sad. I eagerly want to be with them! I can't play here. They've taken away the bodily movement that a child like me needs so much, and also all possible amusement for my eyes. Here I can only look at the Residence's dark and boring walls.

The images start to vanish. They're moving away... I've returned from the past to the present. It has all been so unbelievable. I'm amazed! The scenes from that life were so real. Somehow I entered into a time fold that stores all of the events from that period. It seems as though the connection has ended. A storm is rising, I'll return to the shelter.

Curiosity is eating me away. I've only seen half of the movie. My visions of when I was a little girl were interrupted. I'll return.

Back then, I already had the talent of channelling beings from other dimensions. I think carrying out breathing exercises in this very clean atmosphere, practicing meditation and contemplation, eating healthily and having a balanced diet, living each day with serenity, without stress, and keeping my thoughts positive and transparent, are waking up the talents I had when I was a child.

The Monkeys' Lake

I'm anxious to know more about that past life. I'm going to go back to the rock of the past. It's so great to feel this soft breeze. It's born, it grows, it dies and, suddenly, it's reborn again. It's invisible, but it makes itself apparent. Where were you born? Where are you going? What pushes you? You're so free.

The signs I left along the way have been so very useful. They'll definitely help me to get back to the rock. I should be getting close to the tiled path. Where are the signs? They've disappeared! I don't get it. This is very strange, maybe it was last night's gale... I've lost the clues... I'm going to have to look for it again. I'll put up well-knotted signs next time.

The intense smell is coming from there. Where the vegetation is very leafy and the bushes touch each other, creating a green wall. Here's an entrance. What's this!? It's so fascinating, an empty space surrounded by trees. Their branches touch the ground, forming cascades of beautiful orange flowers. What a breathtaking garden, full of butterflies! They come to... what's the word? Ah, yes, suckle, they come to suckle the flowers. This must be their favorite restaurant.

This place is so special. I'll stay here for some time granting my eyes the pleasure of looking at the butterflies' motion.

"Why do you change direction so much while you're flying? Maybe because you have a lot of predators. Your nomadic flight disorients and discourages them. You've finally found an untouched flower and you intensely dedicate yourself to absorbing its nectar. Wow, it's so good! Dear butterfly, we have some similar basic necessities. You flutter from flower to flower whilst I fly from job to job to get the money that will allow me to fill my cart with the supermarket's nectar. We spend the entire day chasing food."

Never in my life had I seen such exotic butterflies and flowers, with such lively shapes and colors. Ric, where have you brought me? What place is this? It's certainly not my country. It's a shame that I fell asleep during the trip. So many mysterious things...

What... what is it...? I can barely hear it... It's some kind of musical murmur. It sounds like harps and violins, very fine, lingering, without pauses. It goes up and down. Could it be my imagination? Could it be the air going through the cracks in the rock? I can hardly hear it... Now I can hear it better. It's coming from all directions. It's so inspiring.

It's making my soul reach an indefinable state. Could the Deva of Nature, responsible for taking care of this place, be creating it? Could it know I'm here? Could it be dedicating this beautiful music to me? Now a choir of voices has joined. It's giving me goose bumps! Could the choir be its answer, the evidence that the music is a gift for me? I'm not as alone as I thought I was. Well it doesn't matter, whoever you are, thank you for your wonderful melody. I'll always remember this magical moment in this very seductive place.

Hey! Hello, bird friend, what a nice surprise! How did you find me? You've brought me a yellow daisy, today it's almost a bouquet. What a nice gesture! You know how to touch my heart. You're on my shoulder. If I had known that you were coming, I would have brought you a handful of bird seeds. Oh, are you leaving already? Thank you for your gift and for putting it in my hair. I love you.

Going through this thick vegetation is difficult and slow. I puff and pant a lot. What's that bright thing? It glows like the sun's reflection on a mirror. It's a lake!

What clear water! I could bathe in it but it looks icy. It's warm! The lake is completely round. It's in a volcano crater! That's why the water is so warm. Clothes off...

It's so pleasant, like being in an indoor pool, such a luxury. It's so nice to splash around and swim. The deepest part goes up to my waist. It's paradise.

I'm so lucky that I've found this hidden lake. Thank goodness I've marked the route. Now I'll be able to return as many times as I want. I love the feeling of stepping on this very fine sand. I'm going to sunbathe.

It's a joy to feel the sand's warmth and the sunbeams caressing my skin. It's a wonderful experience. I'll stop time... The clouds are moving peacefully. I'm suddenly feeling so sleepy, rocked by the murmur of the waves that touch the shore.

I'm falling in love with this valley, I could stay here forever. I've become fond of everything that surrounds me. Things have changed so much for me. The first few days were difficult. I'm not going to get attached to this place. This is just another phase in my life. I'll have to continue my path in other locations. Meanwhile I'll enjoy the time that I still have here, in this wonderful place, with my heart and senses entirely open.

What an intense smell of flowers! It's a delicious place... I'll be very still savoring the silence, feeling the breeze's caress in my breath, Life within me.

I've been so distanced from nature. How many trees, plants, and flowers names do I know? Very few. How many sunrises and sunsets have I seen during my lifetime? Not many. When have I placidly, deeply put my emotion into them? Never. How much beauty throughout my life, how much creativity, how many feelings lost because I overthought my withered and hasty stories, the ones that pleased my ego, my sorrows... They blurred my mind and vision and stooped my back with their weight, not allowing me to see anything worthwhile. Starting from now I will leave them on the side of the road. Now, I can feel this place from within my soul, my mind, my eyes and my skin, without stories and without hurries! Without hurries! Without hurries! Calmly, from my spirit's peace.

What luck! I've remembered to take my small notebook: *Let's See If I Can Get Some Things Cleared Up*. It might be better if I entitle it *My Inspirational Ideas*, it sounds more elegant. It was a good idea to start to create it. It has some of my reflections, some of my favorite ideas and questions that I still need to solve.

It's like a pointillist painting, one idea here, another over there, spread all over, disorganized. Written in the instant that they appear in my mind, or when they come to me on a tide of knowledge, because they've surprised, intrigued or stimulated me.

It's like a personal book that I'm writing to my liking. It affects me like when I'm feeling apathetic, lazy and I put on some music that changes, stimulates and improves my humor. My reflections are like different flowers in a garden. I stop at each one of them so that I can be captivated by its smell, shapes and colors, and I pause before going to the next one, so that I don't mix the flavors.

I'm so peaceful. It's a good time to read them, to see if I'm absorbing their wisdom:

Love is the power that opens everything, the Universe's grand trick. It nourishes everything. Love always tastes like new. It doesn't tire. Love gives in silence, without asking for anything in return, without expecting a thank you.

I can create gold and diamond or cheap jewelry. It's up to me to choose.

I've received the means to write the script about my life in my own way, with my free will.

Recognizing, listening, being faithful to my Inner Master means saying goodbye to suffering.

I create my reality by directing my attention toward what I want.

My heart, the magic portal.

I am what I eat.

Inner wisdom, I don't know which direction to take. I beg you to guide me.

The beliefs I have today will have been substituted by others tomorrow, created by my growing consciousness, which will get me closer to the truth.

Each time I'm becoming more harmonized with what surrounds me and with myself.

Life, thank you for my mistakes, they also make me grow.

I'm going to leave behind superfluous, useless things so that I'll have more learning capacity.

Everything helps. Even illnesses bring points that can be exchanged for evolutionary prizes.

I'm going to review my mental list of what I need to get rid of and what I need to get.

There's intelligence in all types of Life.

Everything Life receives, it returns multiplied. If you give it flowers, it will give you a garden in return. If you give it dry weeds, a desert.

Love doesn't have an expiry date, a barcode, a price or interest. It's free and always available.

I trust my heart's intuition. It's more precise than my reasoning and my senses.

Between one life and the next there's a resting stop, where you can think about the road you've traveled, and the one you still need to go on.

My life's perspective, its transcendence, changes if I think it's only one of many, a brief blink of my eternal existence.

My thoughts are free. I send them through time and space to where I wish. They're very fast.

I trust Life and its protective power.

If I want to achieve my changes, I need to work on them, but sometimes laziness and apathy triumphs. I take off when I have a materialistic incentive in front of me: success, money, prestige… I step on the gas to reach it, and meanwhile, my high-priority projects: developing my peace, love and consciousness, keep getting delayed because of the time I've lost doing pointless things.

I receive truths when I'm in a pacified and empty mental state.

All of my problems, concerns, fears and sorrows play against me. They go everywhere I go, my inseparable company. They slip in and get comfy in my mental suitcases. When I get to the room in the hotel they come out in a rush, swiftly, getting comfortable in the best places. They don't even give me time to peek through the window. They run to look out of it, pushing in front of me, not allowing me to see the new views. I'll continue to fight against them, so that I can get them away from me.

I'll balance silence and tranquility with action, depending on day-to-day circumstances. I'll focus my attention on the tasks I am working on presently, without allowing my mind to be distracted by the future. That will increase the joy, learning, stimulus, incentive in my life. Everything in its own time.

I won't know the taste of an apple if, while I'm eating it, I'm thinking about what the orange in front of me tastes like. And if when I eat the orange I try to remember the flavor of the apple, I won't know what either of them taste like. If my attention is ahead of the action or lagging behind, I won't know what the movie is about.

I won't forget that experiences are teachers that show me how to continue moving towards the summit. I chose and planned them, even if I have forgotten. If I don't like them, I know who I need to complain to.

It looks like those bush's branches have moved! I can't tell what it is. They're on the far side of the lake. Yes, again, there are animals in them! My heart jumps. What are they? They're monkeys! There are five of them, a couple, two babies and another one that the mother is carrying in her arms. I'm afraid. Some monkeys are aggressive. They could attack me. I'm going to overcome my fear, by sending them love energy, and maybe it will get rid of their possible suspicion, agitation, hostility...

They've seen me. They watch me without coming near, keeping their distance. Maybe they're more frightened than me. They're going toward the water and getting into it.

They're enjoying their bath. The two younger ones bother their mother tirelessly. They climb on her, hanging off her and then getting off. She patiently deals with them, making sure that they don't touch the newborn she's got in her arms and hurt it by slapping or hitting it while they play. Every time they try to touch it she gently pushes them away, but when they don't listen to her she shows them her teeth. My eyes meet with hers and a spark of understanding jumps between us. They're having a great time! They go underwater and when they come up they shake their heads vigorously from one side to the other to dry themselves.

They get some stems and eat them. They clean them in the water before eating them! They look at me from time to time without fear or agitation. They must be thinking: "What is this usurper doing in our lake? What a strange monkey! She doesn't have hair on her body. She must feel cold sometimes." They're cautiously getting closer to me. They want to see me up close. I'm their remarkable show and they're mine. Sending them love seem to have worked. I have new friends. I'll return often to visit them. I asked the Universe for someone to talk to and they're its answer. They do it in their own way, with their language, their eyes, their mimicking, their attention and with their personality. Their eyes reflect their intelligence.

What does the male have entangled in his hair? One of my ribbon signs! The mystery of the disappearance of the signs that took me to *The Rock of the Past* is solved.

"Why did you stay behind? Why haven't you evolved like humans have? Did your vocal chords fail? Language goes hand-in-hand with knowledge and evolution. Did you communicate telepathically? Did you think that you didn't need language? Did you lack a Loo-chi-chi? Don't worry, you're on the right path.

Sorry but I have to leave. A storm is rising and I need to get to the shelter before it gets dark. I'll see you as soon as I can. Your desire to live and sociability have filled my heart. Your company has been a treat for my loneliness. You're beautiful. I love you. Next time I'll bring you hazelnuts and I'll confide in you. Already, before leaving, I'm missing you. Oh, I need to ask you for a favor: don't remove my route signs. I'll tie them better"

Did the invisible delivery man bring the supplies? "Refrigerator open." Yes, they're here! I have to admit that the biggest wonder in this shelter has to be how the supplies get into the refrigerator, I can't explain it. It's pure magic, but it works great. It's a brilliant, unlikely technology, a dream-like system. I love its simplicity. I open the refrigerator, and when I least expect it, magically, the food has already arrived! It's full, with everything well organized, and it's free! It's so fascinating!

What abundance! There's so much color! It looks like an impressionist painting, *Fruits and vegetables*. Let's see what else we have here… Nuts… with a free nutcracker, perfect. This food is very good. The truth is that Ric is spending a lot of money. He sends me the healthiest food. Of course, being vegetarian, I save him some money. What a nice box! What could it be? It looks like a gift. It's wrapped-up in a golden, glistening paper and it's decorated with a lot of different colored ribbons, which form beautiful bows. What could it be? Could it be a cake? What are you saying, crazy woman! The person who made the package loves tomatoes, zucchini, onions… No, he doesn't have that type of refinement. It could be a cauliflower, well presented, to change its normal appearance.

What can I do with these multicolored ribbons? I don't want to throw them away. They're so bright. It's going to take me awhile to untangle them. Ah, I know! They'll look nice hanging from the branches of a tree. The sun will brighten up their color. Will the birds get scared when they see them blowing in the wind? They won't care. They do their own thing, gorging their little stomachs with seeds.

I'm so impatient unwrapping paper! I can't believe it! A cake! This is something Ric would do. A sentence written in chocolate. "Be happy in the valley, Eva." What a delightful gift! I see it, but I don't believe it. It's so beautiful, it's so beautiful! Thank you, Ric… The excitement has made me cry. And I was raving against you in the valley. Sorry, Ric, I had some bad moments. I love you. Thank you for your tasty gift. Also, thanks gift packer. I'll eat it in your health's honor.

It's the hour of truth. Taste glands ready. Concentration at extreme level. Clean fingers. Teeth ready to chew. I don't want to miss anything about this surprising event. A day is a day…

Let's see what plan I can come up with for today. I'll spend some time reading the book that I started yesterday, while I sunbathe.

"Okay, okay… Good morning, my little bird friends. You're coming toward me in a flock. You were waiting for me. Are you coming to say hello to me or to remind me that you're hungry? Do you know what I'm telling you? One of these days I'm going to get a note with Ric's supplies saying: You're not in a zoo, you're spoiling them. They're going to forget to look for their food. They'll put on weight and become lazy and inactive."

Okay, that's enough already. Don't run over each other, there's enough for everyone. Don't pile on one another, you're getting on top of each other. When you see food you forget your good manners. It's my fault, I was distracted and I've given you seeds in a small space rather than spreading it out. You remind me of when I was a child and my grandma would take me to street fairs. High up in the floats people would throw a bunch of candies everywhere. All the kids would rush desperately to grab them from the ground, pushing each other over, just like you're doing right now. It's more or less the same.

My grandma and I would get back home with our pockets full of candies. Then my grandma would say to me: "You need your teeth for the rest of your life, so we will distribute them among the children in the neighborhood."

I agreed in a foul mood, complaining and with a frown on my face. She would always say to me: "You eat sugar and the sugar eats your teeth. If you continue this way, when you're older I can see you setting up a camping tent in the dentist's office."

Little birds, I'll let you eat calmly. I'm going to stretch out my legs, even though you don't care... When you're eating you don't pay attention to anyone.

The little animals share this immense paradise with me. The squirrels, the birds, the butterflies, the lizards know that I'm here. They contemplate me, pay attention to me. They keep me in mind, evaluating me, counting on me. "What a strange animal! But we like her. Welcome to the little animals' club." They've accepted me as one more in their valley's casino. "The new tenant of the junk shelter." They don't forget me, they remember me, and they come back to me.

Thank you, dear creatures, for your presence, for soothing my solitude.

They have a heart. They suffer, enjoy, fear... They know how to measure my love or my fear. They're not bewildered or sleepy, but very awake, perceptive, vibrant...

Their wisdom amazes me. They're born with all of their script learned, with the program ready, up-to-date. They know how to act in each moment, without doubting themselves. Their genetic encyclopedia does wonders for them and they trust it. They've improved it. They've been attending Life's classes for millions of years without missing a single day.

Bread... Sun... Live... Be

I'm impatient. I need to find *The Rock of the Past*. I'll begin the search again.

There's so much life under my feet. When I walk on the bushes and dead leaves and the bugs and insects that live underneath feel the vibration of my footsteps, they flee so that they won't get stepped on. I need to be as careful as possible not to step on them, hurt them or make them feel that they're being attacked so that they retaliate.

I suppose if I see a wild boar it will turn around and go away, unless I accidentally go into its den and it thinks that its entrance has been blocked and it can't escape. Or if it's with its piglets, it could attack me in order to defend them. Usually, animals have a very well-tuned instinct and they know when a person is aggressive or trustworthy.

I feel so fulfilled! I'm so happy sensing how my calm breathing is filling my lungs with cosmic energies. Thank you, Sun, for your warmth, for your gleaming light which makes everything it touches happy. I'm rediscovering the world as seen through the eyes of a child, who's delighted with everything and impatient to see the world she's discovering. Delicious! This slice of tasty oiled wheat bread fills me with happiness. It's exquisite. Bread... Sun... Live... Be. It's an extreme luxury.

The great moments that I'm living in this paradise. The deep peace, contemplation, breathing take me to quiet mental states that evoke memories, internal rebirths...

This is great. The news downpour doesn't reach this paradise. In the city, because of the book translation, I avoided a lot of the news flooding. Still, they invaded my sight, ears and mind, leaving behind a trail that gradually went away.

I find it easy to leave my ideas behind in this silent kingdom. I do this by simply sitting down and whispering to my mind: "You've earned yourself a break. I'm freeing you from your elaborate thoughts. Take as much time as you want to enter an empty mental state that will favor your quietness."

My ideas and my eyesight are clarified by pacifying my mind. Every time I see something I'll take off it's "I've already seen it" wrapper, and I'll look at it differently, as if it were the first time I'd seen it, looking at all of its different features, intensifying my vision. I don't want things to go unnoticed because I've looked at them so much I no longer see them, like what happened in the camel story:

"Have you seen this camel?

"A camel? No, I haven't seen any camel today, where is it?"

"Here, it's next to you."

"Oh! This is my camel. It's always with me."

This is life. I'm learning from animals who can have a great time without spoiling their good moments with unimportant things.

I've never valued Life so much as now. Wherever I look I see it: in lizards, bumblebees, flowers… Everything lives and grows with delight. I've always been fascinated by how crystals develop, adopting geometrical shapes, so perfect, so clear and translucent, resembling a bouquet of flowers or diamonds. Who's the jeweler that makes them grow? In this living valley I admire, more than ever, the great creativity that nature has.

You know what, Life, I don't demand anything from you. I know that you always offered me the best things for my development. You've been immensely splendid. You haven't given me a limited time. You've given me an endless, eternal existence. I'll always be able to explore brighter and brighter spaces, where my spirit will continue elevating and improving its Light.

"Diligent little bird, I've been watching you poking around for a long time, untiringly, with your beak in that tree trunk's hole. Ah! You're probably trying to get a larva hidden at bottom, but you can't reach it. Your beak is too short. You try and try again, desperately hoping to reach the little worm. You have a lot of patience. You've been at it for a long time, non-stop. You must be thinking: "This is so annoying! If I had a longer beak I would gorge myself by eating larvae. I could take heaps of worms to my hungry hatchlings. Why can't I have a longer beak? I want to have a longer beak. I need to have a longer beak, longer than a hummingbird's. I want to have a longer beak to gorge myself with larvae, I want…"

I'm sure your cells, fed up with receiving the same desire so many times, think: "The boss is irritating. Let's move around so that he can leave us alone." So they start to work to satisfy your eager ambition, and because they're so intelligent and hard-working they achieve it. That intense desire of wanting a longer beak will make your next generation have their beaks a bit longer. "That's great. It will be my gift for my next generation. It will come from me, through my genetic mail. They'll be able to gorge themselves on a lot of larvae."

Necessity creates the organ. The persistent desire during each generation, century after century, makes the miracle happen: the little bird becomes its own designer, but it's very likely that its descendants will continue wanting it. "As my beak gets longer the larvae hide deeper within the trunk. They're clever like squirrels. I need a longer beak." Is it like that? It could be. I live in a magical world, but I didn't realize it. I've lost a lot of time looking at myself in the mirror. I've barely started to reflect about this topic and many others. I'm not too sure about them. Maybe I am simplifying it too much, I need to get more information. I'll get up to date. I'll copy the little bird's tenacity.

This hat is more than a hat, it's like a parasol. It's a good thing it was in the shelter, it protects me when the burning sun falls vertically. It's not healthy to have so much heat on your head. With the damaged ozone layer, it's not wise to expose myself to the sunbeams for a lot of time or to look at it directly. Its light is more intense than it used to be and it could hurt my eyes. It might be better to enjoy its caresses with moderation, when it's not too hot, ideally in the early morning and late evening.

There are so many delicate balls floating in the air. They're smaller than a golf ball. The sun's rays go through them and lights them up. They're so light that they allow the wind to choose their direction. They let themselves be carried away, enjoying the beautiful images that the valley is showing them along the way.

The quietness of this place is helping me to contemplate my thoughts with more clarity and to choose the most useful and transparent. Little by little I'm taming my mind's wild horse.

It's a good time and place to take a glance at *My Prodigious Changes List*:

I write down my changes in the present instead of the future, as if they were positive affirmations. In other words, instead of: *I'll stop... I'll sleep... I'll dedicate...* I write: *I stop... I sleep... I dedicate...* This immediacy gives them strength and effectiveness. Here I go:

I leave behind all of my past stage without bitterness, with love. I'm grateful to the people that I've met during my life, because they have shown me my path.

I stop my impatience, and move forward little-by-little so that I can enjoy all of the road's details without hurrying.

When I'm not too sure about my decisions I let them rest for awhile, so that I can contemplate them with more clarity when I find them again.

I want to clean my mind, leave it sparkling and transparent, occupied with only positive and useful thoughts.

I don't flee from difficult situations. I confront them, feel them, internalize them and dedicate time to resolve them.

When I do the daily tasks that need little attention, I can practice one of the changes that I want to introduce into my life. For example, while I'm waiting for the bus or walking down the street I'll enjoy my breathing, the pleasure of feeling its gentle caress on my chest, or I'll maintain a good posture, or I'll contemplate the life that surrounds me, elevating my capacity for perception. While doing housework I'll do my chores calmly, listening to, or singing mantras or saying positive affirmations...

I don't sleep for too long so that I don't wake up feeling tired, rigid and stiff.

Once in awhile, I dedicate some time to go over *My Prodigious Changes List*, to keep it up to date and not to forget my new and good intentions.

I get rid of useless activities. That way I'll have more free time to do what I like: read, daydream, meditate, go for a walk in nature, expand my knowledge, listen to music, dance, whistle, talk with my friends, contemplate birds as they fly...

There are changes that don't need time, energy or money to integrate them: the intention and will is enough. For example, I avoid arguments, cook simple meals, set my alarm early, think without nourishing depressing ideas...

I ask the Universe to bring abundance into my life.

I wait before speaking, without interrupting, until the person finishes what he is saying.

I stop interfering in other people's business. Everyone deals with their own problems. Their tasks are the lessons that Life presents them in order to learn. By helping, I am depriving them of the opportunity to grow. It's like doing a child's homework for him, he'll learn less. It's another matter to help someone who asks for it and really needs it.

I am dragging a lot of habits, beliefs, norms, styles, obsolete teachings, along with me. They delay my advancement so I will leave them behind, replacing them with behaviors that advance my growth.

I get strength from my inner warrior. She helps me start my changes, silently, cordially and efficiently.

I feel life from my heart, expanding my inner and external horizons, avoiding static positions.

I keep practicing meditation, confronting my comforts, my weaknesses, my hurries… Why am I so impatient? I'm eternal.

I observe myself with truth, internally and externally, so that I can discover my defects and limitations, and gradually correct them, transforming them into qualities.

I strengthen my desire to achieve *my prodigious changes* and I keep practicing them until I integrate them.

I avoid watering my ego, polishing theatre lights. Who cares if there's dust on my boots if my eyes are full of dawns and my heart is overflowing with stars?!

I light the wick of the rocket of antagonism and triviality. I hope they go very far and never return.

I see everything just like a little girl would, like a premiere, with my heart sparkling in my eyes.

I forgive myself when I'm late, when I fall, when I don't arrive, when I throw in the towel. I know that after low and discouraging moments I will get up again. I won't give up. I will pick it up as many times as I throw it in and I know I'll get there eventually.

I'm not distracted by consumerism like a baby with his rattle.

I listen from my heart, silently and quietly, to Life, that dissolves environmental interferences and gives me the answers to my questions.

I fertilize and water the patience, which drop by drop elevates stalactite cathedrals in caverns, and the creativity, which moves icebergs.

My old comfort zone, ignorance and mediocrity, no longer satisfies me. Go away fear of change!

I open myself up to new airs even if they disassemble my unstable platform of comfort and the well-known. I'm embracing the new challenges that strong gales rise, that sweep-up my rancid habits and my obsolete beliefs. My inner warrior welcomes them with open arms, and she goes through the recently discovered routes full of courage, joy, tolerance, strength, wisdom, serenity, peace, love…

It seems easy to take a look at *My Prodigious Changes List*, even if it's only for a few minutes a day. However, often a few days pass before I consult it again. Maybe I unconsciously relate it to work, with obligations that require more effort and less comfort.

The word soup was delicious, it's left a good mind after-taste.

Another day to enjoy life! What a special light and revitalizing cool air! This invigorating wind is full of fragrances.

Today, I'm going to try to contemplate and see things as children do. They lack time to see everything. They don't want to miss any of the games and adventures that life puts before them in each moment. I'll forget about myself and delightfully sink into the fascinating world that surrounds me.

An infinity of tiny yellow flowers are falling from that tree, knitting a carpet over the ground. The sun goes through them, transforming them into a shower of little golden lights.

I've stepped on an anthill! I feel so guilty. I've destroyed it, poor ants. They're probably yelling at me: "We don't know if you can hear our voices from up there. Look what you've done. Why are you so clumsy? Is it so difficult for you to look where you're stepping, and not squash or trip over us? If you step on some sleeping bug, you will irritate it and it could bite you. Go away and don't ever return." "Forgive me. I'm so sorry. From now on I'll look where I step."

Looking at a beautiful landscape of mountains from far away is one thing and being close to it is another story. Being surrounded by insects and bugs: flies, ants, wasps, mosquitoes… has its problems and its dangers. Their small size is deceiving. I'm not going to underestimate tiny insects, for example ants, there are very poisonous species in some countries, and their bite can be very serious. I'll keep them in mind and disturb them as little as possible. I'll watch where I lean my foot or my butt, to avoid sitting on an anthill. I'll always be alert, not distracted as I was in the city.

I won't forget about the bigger animals either. I won't bother them or enter their territory. If they feel threatened or in danger they could attack.

I'm aware that I would be defenceless against them. I'm in a weaker position. What chances would I have against a tiger, a lion or a hungry bear? They've been trained over millions of years to attack. I would be safe inside a four-by-four or with a weapon to scare them or to defend myself if they attacked me.

I hope that there aren't any dangerous animals around here. So far I haven't seen any... I'm not going to obsess over it. There are risks everywhere. The key is to reduce them by taking appropriate measures, not over the top, being careful to a certain point, otherwise I would never leave the shelter. I trust that, with the protective power of Life, everything will go okay for me. However, I also collaborate by taking the appropriate measures.

From now on, every time I go out I will take the shepherd's cane with me. Ric told me it would be very helpful, that I should always go out with it. It could be useful if I need to drive away an aggressive animal. Besides, it's also great for brushing away the spider webs between the bushes as I move along, and to lean on it when I'm climbing steep terrain.

One of the ways that things could go wrong is if I become impatient to see them finished. If I travel along a path nervous and heedlessly, I could hit myself with a branch, trip, fall, go over a cliff... If I get lost I could wander around for days until I found the shelter, if I find it. It could be very difficult if I were caught up in a storm without equipment and a place to protect myself. I'm learning from the animals. They never let their guard down. They're always alert. Birds are always watching to see if any predators are getting close so that they have enough time to escape.

I need to have a philosophy so that nature is pleasant to me. Minimize the nuisances and risks that bother me. In the city I also have to deal with mosquitoes, flies, ants, cockroaches, acarus and many more.

Bumblebee, your technique is incredible. You fly from one flower to the next. Your speed is so vertiginous that you almost disappear in your trajectory. You drastically stop and suspend yourself in the air, still, right in front of the flower's appetizing nectar. Your art amazes me! The control you have when you fly is astounding. You've distracted me from my meditation practice. You know what, it's starting to work! I'm able to keep practicing it. Everyday I dedicate some time to it. I'm noticing results: I'm calmer, I have more inner peace, my fears have lessened, my ideas are clearer, I'm more self-confident. My sorrows don't haunt me as much as they used to. I'm sweeping my unreal realities away and embracing my real unrealities.

What a beautiful place! The air is so pure. It's a delight to feel how the air enters and exits my chest, like a soft tide. A slow wave comes, caressing me with love, and it calmly withdraws itself, always coming and going with the same rhythm. I savor the air's oxygen and prana. They're reparative, invigorating, inspiring... Breathing makes me peaceful, quieting my mind and connecting me with the Universe's beat.

I'm so well. It's the perfect moment to say some positive affirmations. So that they're more effective I'll repeat them by believing in them, with my heart's yearning. I think that words, just like thoughts, are energies that act. Therefore, they have the capacity to heal and change my life, to bring me happiness, fulfillment, whatever I desire... I say the affirmations in the present because it gives them strength. Instead of I will be successful, I say: I am successful, I am success, success accompanies me...

I avoid saying no or using negative terms because, apparently, the subconscious doesn't perceive it. It suppresses it. It takes I don't lie as I lie. Instead, I say: I am truthful. Instead of I am not nervous, I say: I am calm.

In lotus posture, I relax my whole body. I breathe through my nose. Every time I inhale and exhale I repeat the affirmation. Focusing all of my attention on it, and fervently maintaining it in my mind will make it become a reality. If during the exercise I watch out for intrusive thoughts, so that they don't interfere, it will almost become a meditation practice. Let's see what affirmation I can come up with... I am healthy. Okay. Inhaling. *I am healthy.* Exhaling. *I am healthy.* Inhaling. *I am healthy...*

I can also change affirmations as I go, repeating each one several times:

I am peace and I emit peace. I am peace and I emit peace...
My thoughts are positive. My thoughts...
I am the joy and happiness of living. I am the joy...
I am economic abundance. I am economic...
My mind is serene and strong. My mind is serene and strong...
I thank Life for my life. I thank Life...
I am nature, humility and strength. I am...

I can say or think the affirmations one after another:

I keep myself young. I am happy. I am healthy. I am fulfillment. I am serenity and peace. I am increasing my consciousness. I take care of my body and my mind. I am faithful to myself. I am love and I love. I am light and I illuminate. I am peace and I pacify. I think, speak and act calmly. I live without judging, comparing, criticizing. I am protected by Life. I am in harmony. I am a precious being. My thoughts are pure, true, useful, and joyful. I live with my mind in the present, distanced from the past and the future. I inhale Light, I fill my body with Universe Light...

I have my affirmations list up-to-date, crossing out the ones that are done and adding new ones.

I'm Eva Luz

It's not bad. I already have several itineraries marked: *The Butterflies' Sanctuary*, *The Deva's Musical Circus*, *The Monkeys' Lake*... but I still haven't found *The Rock of the Past*. I'll continue exploring... I'll take an unknown route.

Aaaah, I've hit my head against that stupid branch. I'm sorry branch, it's not your fault. It's your territory. I came along and bumped into you because I was thinking about my own problems. I shouldn't be day dreaming. There aren't any emergency points here. I'm going to walk around with all of my senses concentrating on what I'm doing, on what surrounds me, with my mind in the present, not in uncertain pasts or futures, or solving mental crosswords.

What a drastic weather change! A hurricane has just risen. There are large black clouds as dark as coal covering the sun. There's going to be heavy rain. I'd better go back to the shelter as fast as I can. I'm going to get moving so that the storm doesn't catch me. I can see the shelter, I have about ten minutes to get there. The clouds have covered the sun. There's no light... It looks like nighttime. The wind's roar is scary. It's impressive to see how the gale violently shakes the trees' branches, breaking the weakest ones. Its gusts almost knock me down! It's started to rain a lot. What a big water curtain! It's getting worse. Oh, nooo! It's hidden the shelter. I don't have any more references. Rocks, trees, heaths, bushes, everything looks the same to me. I don't know what direction I should go in. How will I guide myself? With this darkness I can't see where the return signals are. I should have taken the equipment. I still haven't worn it. I'm freezing with only this t-shirt on. The temperature is probably dropping to less than zero degrees. Who would have said it this morning when it was so hot? The gale continues to get worse. If I don't find the shelter soon I'm lost. I don't know if I'm getting closer or further away from it.

It's raining a lot. I'm soaked. I'm trembling, even my hair shivers. Great, just what I needed, the fog is getting thicker, diminishing my vision even more. I'm moving by touching surfaces. Ahhh! What a skid! The ground is muddy and slippery. I need to move forward staying entirely alert so that I don't fall, or I could go over a cliff.

If I have to spend the night outside I'll freeze to death like a little bird would. I'm not going to lose hope! Fears go away! No negative thoughts! The mind is creative. I'm going to think positively. I'm not going to give in. I'll get out of this one. I'll find the shelter. I won't give up. I'm going to keep on moving so that my blood circulates. Stopping means becoming drowsy, freezing, dying...

Nooo! It's starting to hail. They're as big as almonds. They're painful, I'm going to get bruised! I'll protect my head with my hands. This gigantic tree's branches slow down the hail, so it hits me with less strength.

The hail is making so much noise. This is such an intimidating scenario. I'm not going to stay still. I'm going to keep on moving my legs and arms. It's so cold, so unbearable! My teeth are rattling like castanets...

How much time could have passed? An eternity! It could have just been half an hour. It's going to be difficult to find the shelter. It's like finding a needle in a hay stack... in an ocean of mountains. Only a miracle will help me find it. A miracle! With so much commotion going on, I've forgotten to ask for help. Creator, light friends, grandma... I can't see you but I know you're there and you're listening to me. You can see the desperate situation I'm in. Please, guide me to the shelter. Let's see what you can come up with, I'm in a severe situation. I'm freezing to death, don't take too long. Thank you.

The hailstorm has stopped, I'll continue moving... Every time I fall I hit myself and it takes me a century to get up. I fear falling into a void. I'm walking blindly, touching everything with my hands and feet. It would probably be better if I crawl on all fours. The fog is partly responsible for the total darkness. Inner Wisdom, I know that you can join your forces with the team that's guiding me to the shelter...

I've been sliding over wet stones for an eternity. It's like being in an ice rink, falling, hitting myself against rocks and bushes. My body is all bruised. I can't handle it anymore. I'm losing strength, exhausted, shivering. My hands and feet are so numb I can barely feel them. If I survive I'll always take the equipment with me and lay some rope out so that I can find my way back. I've never liked to travel with loads, but here the equipment means life. Who would have said this morning, when it was so sunny, what has happened.?

I'm becoming drowsy. I'll slap myself. I can't stop moving so I'll keep walking... What's touching my face? It's jelly-like, soft, like seaweed. The wind is entangling it with my hair. Oh! It's one of the plastic ribbons that decorated my cake box and that I tied to a tree's branches! Hooray, hooray! I'm only fifty feet away from the shelter! Thank you, Universe, thank you all for your help, for the life saving ribbons.

How can I know where the shelter is? It's completely dark. If I go the wrong way I can disorient myself and I'll get lost again. Instead of getting closer I could move further away. What do I do? I'm so close to salvation. Universe, continue helping me put light in my mind... "Light" translated means luz! Eva Luz! "I'm Eva Luz." The code to activate the sensor to open the door. Once it opens, the interior brightness will transform it into a ray of light. I'll have to shout loudly so that the rain's splashing and the winds don't obstruct my words. Here I go. "I'm Eva Luz"... it's not opening. Maybe it doesn't identify me because my voice is hoarse.

Now is the moment! The winds' racket has decreased. This time, I will be lucky. "I'm Eva Luz." Stronger. "I'm Eva Luz..." Ah! Yes, yes, yes, yessss! Bravo, bravo, bravo! It has opened completely. You can see its interior light. A ray of light in the darkness. I can't hold back my tears. They're mixing with the rain. Thank you God and all of your aides.

I'm limping, as if I was returning from a war. I'm wrecked, but I'm still alive! My knees are failing. I fall down. I move by crawling, dripping mud. Welcome, it's healing. I'm going in. Wow! It's so warm. "Door close." I'm dripping wet. Clothes off. I'll dry and rub myself to get warmer, so that my blood circulation can recover its normality. "Temperature twenty-five." I'm full of injuries, bruises, and scratches. I'll cut a leaf from this Aloe Vera cactus and rub myself with its pulp, it will be good for me and will heal my wounds. "No sound, level ten." The noise and the coldness of the storm have stayed outside. What comforting silence!

Everything is so magical. Whoever decorated the cake with ribbons saw more than me, they saw the future. The cake wasn't the gift, the ribbons were. They carried a great present, my life. When I went to go throw away the box and the ribbons, an idea popped into my mind: "They'll look very nice hanging from a tree." Later on my ego took control over it and added: "I'll tie these beautiful colored ribbons on a tree's branches, in front of the shelter, I imagine them waving around with the wind. What a wonderful idea I've just had. I have a great imagination." I couldn't have imagined that hanging them would have saved my life. Thank you, Ric, for insisting that I activate the voice recognition command to open the front door.

I couldn't see far ahead. No! I had forgotten! When I was hanging the ribbons I had a quick vision: I had a ribbon entangled in my hair under heavy rain...

My point of view has changed, I used to think that I faced situations alone. Now I know that, on occasions, they take me by the hand and, sometimes, they carry me in their arms. Life cares, protects, like parents do with their children: they give them freedom, so that they can learn from solving their own problems. They don't take away their lessons, so that they can develop their own initiative, self-confidence and talent, but they watch over and help them when they surpass an acceptable level of risk.

In the past, I would have thought: "I'm letting my imagination fly. I'm creating a fictional story. Everything that's happened has all been coincidence." Now I don't believe in coincidences. This adventure has been difficult, but at the same time it's been magical and influential.

There's not a single calendar. What day could it be today? I still don't have minutes or days. It's so liberating, not having an agenda, telephone, TV, radio, magazines, and cell phone. Without Saturdays or Sundays. Every day is a holiday! The birds don't seem to need the equipment either. So far I haven't seen any of their nests with a TV or calendar hanging from a branch. Ha, I'm so funny. Where shall I walk to today? Look for the rock of the past, of course. I don't even want to think about it. My entire body hurts from yesterday's adventure. I'll stay in the valley to recover my strength. I'll look around the shelter to see if I can find a new surprise and then I'll meditate and do some yoga postures. I'll listen to what the birds tell each other. I'll admire the flowers...

What a beautiful squirrel! It's attentively observing me from its high, privileged position in the tree. "What attracts you to me?" It slowly descends. It comes toward me with caution, stopping, thinking about it.

"Do you think I'm dangerous? Why are you coming toward me? Ah! You can smell the intoxicating smell of the hazelnuts I'm eating. To earn your trust I'll throw one at you. You've caught it really quickly with your front paws. You devour it with a lot of fervor. You start to get closer again. Your hunger has conquered your fear and prudence. Hey! Where are you going? Don't even dream about it, stop! Stop going up my pant's leg. You've quickly checked me out and you think I'm completely harmless. The hazelnut has made you my friend and partner. Get down! You haven't paid attention to me. You've gone up all the way to my shoulder. You can't control your hunger for these scrumptious hazelnuts.

From up there you're obsessively looking at my hand full of tasty hazelnuts. You've never tasted them toasted. I don't need to know your next move. You're going to go down my arm until you reach my hand, the supply warehouse. Hey! In a blink of an eye you've become part of the consumerist society. It's a system that fascinates you, from the supermarket to your mouth. You've loved the fact that you didn't have to find and crack a hazelnut on your own."

"Life, you're introducing me to so many messengers to cheer me up, to resist the call from the city and the waves of loneliness that I get in this beautiful but so extremely remote and solitary place."

I'm going to reflect for awhile, I'll choose a complicated and touchy subject: thoughts.

"Thoughts, thoughts… Are you my friends or my enemies? Sometimes you caress me and other times you slap me. Listen up! In my mind I only want peace. From now on, you, the "hitters", are no longer welcomed, you'll find the entrance door closed."

It's clear that some of my thoughts are responsible for decreasing my will to live and surrounding me with sadness and depression. They dominate me. They have the key to my laughter and my tears. If I could control them I would make them useful, transparent, positive, pure, optimistic, creative... and I would put an end to my sorrows.

My learning method is easy: live the experiences that life puts before me and reflect upon them. What happens is that the flood of worthless thoughts that visits me, without giving me peace, leaves me without free time to consider these experiences clearly, without turbulences.

My mind creates my reality. It's up to me whether I create futile thoughts or valuable thoughts. Let's see if I can understand it better. I'll give myself an example: I'm at a party next to the appetizer table, eating with my mouth full. I yell at a person that I know on the other side of the room, who is cheerily talking in a group. He sees me calling him over and he comes toward me. I throw myself in his arms and cover him with kisses. He's delighted with my wonderful greeting and signs-up for another one.

Okay, my mind acts the same way, just like when I call my friend. If it calls happiness, happiness will listen and come, if it calls health, the same thing will happen, and if it calls economic abundance, the same thing will occur... that's how it works.

My thoughts create my reality, it's that simple... But if I don't believe it, it won't work. If I had called my friend at the party by whispering his name, the noise at the party would have prevented him from hearing it and he would have continued to talk. Basically, this whole messy example has been to explain to myself, with more or less luck, that the mind is creative. Today I've eaten an ABC soup. I liked the kisses' greeting example.

I focus my mind on crystalline, lucid, useful things, instead of disorientating it with silly things. Let's see if I don't forget. One thing is to say it and another is to do it.

Having a quiet mind, controlling my thoughts, watching over them and choosing the best ones throughout the day helps to make them better, purer and ensures that they come from the real me, from my Inner Wisdom. This way they'll heal my body and make it younger.

My disturbing thoughts are used to moving freely all over the place, messing everything up, without accepting any type of control. They aren't going to like it when I put fences in front of them, preventing them from entering my mind, altering everything.

Most of my thoughts don't belong to my soul. They're foreigners who've subtly been attached to me along my path, by society, by the media, by people, by my environment, by my genes... I'm tired of them. They irritate me and cause me problems. They waste my energy and time. They manipulate, frighten and control me. They're at the front of the line and I'm at the end of it. I'll do some cleaning. I'll only keep the genuine ones, the ones that are really mine, the ones that make me feel good, improve, smile... I take out the ones that bother me and put them outside the door, locking it behind me.

If I detect an unhelpful thought I'll automatically substitute it for a positive one, for an optimistic affirmation, for a mantra or a song. If I change my thoughts my life will change.

Having a quiet and serene mind, without hurries, helps me perceive and discard undesirable thoughts that haunt me.

I need to organize my mind by getting rid of the thoughts that bother me, that take up the space reserved for essential thoughts, which in turn are tired of waiting for a free space where they could be listened to and be useful.

If my mind is moving back and forth in the future or the past, I'll miss out on the wonderful present and interpret my role very poorly.

Crowded in front of my mind's drawbridge, a multitude of entangled opportunistic thoughts await, hoping I might neglect my attention and lower it so that they can sneak in. It is an unruly crowd. They step on top of one another, impatient and eager to take the leading role.

I'm controlling my mind a lot more. Problematic thoughts are slipping in less and less. It's nice to have it that way. A few months ago they controlled my mind, steering me. They turned it over, disturbed, stepped on it... Now it's me. I'm becoming the director of my fine mental symphonies. I'm transforming their collection of obsolete hisses into celestial music.

Well, mind, my friend. Now you and I are going to take a walk. If you behave yourself and you don't discolor the landscapes by obscuring them with your colorless stories, as a prize I'll give you a box of chocolates full of your favorite thoughts.

In these mountains, the city's display windows have become sunsets. Here, I've substituted everyone's applauses for my own. Now I paint my landscapes, instead of criticizing the one's other people create.

I'm starting over. I'm going to take my path with a different attitude. Everything else is staying behind. They've been phases and they've helped me. I forgive myself and I forgive others. I begin without leaving behind any pending matter.

We go together, but I know that I'm on a solitary voyage. Only I, with effort and dedication, can increase my level of consciousness to expand my understanding of Creation. I'll walk delightedly with the sun and Life's breeze, with my senses open and my mind full of light. The future is now. The seeds I'm planting right now will be tomorrow's flowers. Everything helps.

There are thousands of rocks spread over this extensive plain. They look organized, you can walk among them. Their surface is covered with drawings. It's astonishing, a rock library.

They come in all sizes. Some of them must weigh tons. What a huge task! Who could have drawn such a detailed, enormous quantity of data? Why? For whom?

I sense they were chiseled with emotion by humans who wanted to share their dreams, knowledge, discoveries or doubts with those who would arrive in the future and would find them. An extraordinary legacy with an immeasurable human and scientific value. I don't understand how a civilization with so few resources could have left such advanced messages. Did they receive them from travelers that came from outer space? Were they the scribes, offering their knowledge to future generations?

This historical evidence reminds us how provisional we really are, and yet we continue with our arrogance.

It was a civilization that became extinct. It disappeared, like many others, leaving their messages recorded on rocks, a material that has resisted over time. They used them as support, as notepads to engrave their knowledge on. They inscribed them with only drawings, without writing, using very schematic, clean images. A universal language so that everyone could understand.

On this large rock you can see short individuals standing next to tall, thin and big-headed beings. Could they have been space travelers who used helmets to protect themselves from the Earth's atmosphere? Was their mission to teach and help the residents, less advanced than them? I don't know… a lot of civilizations could have existed since the Earth started to rotate millions of years ago.

Maybe our civilization, like the one of the rock library, is receiving, from other worlds, advances and knowledge. Perhaps they transmit it, drop by drop, as we reach a consciousness that is more prepared to use it with wisdom and humanity.

"I'll have a conversation with you, bird friend. I know you're listening to me. You, Life or my Inner Master's inspiration will put the words into my mind." I'll take in some pacifying breaths and I'll lower my quiet mind to my heart to make it more receptive.

"Can you, bird friend, tell me why your songs are so joyful?"

"They come from the force that dwells within me, giving me another day to sing."

"Why are you in such a hurry? What moves you?"

"The desire to reach my bright inner landscapes."

"Aren't you worried that, with your hasty flapping, you will get exhausted and you will be left without anything?"

"Without anything? And what about the dazzling sunrises, the countless stars and the magical musical breezes? Backpacks made of precious stones break your back and make you constantly thirsty.

Flying to the far mountain is a bitter-sweet experience, but, thanks to this effort, we receive so many sunrises on the summit.

It's a program without a remote control. It's called: *Casting off Ropes*, using the wedding sails for the first time, without mending or unstitching. They've been kept away for a long time. The time

169

is now. Leave behind arks and chests full of moldy memories and spider webs. Now is the time to move onward.

It's another epic. Take your foot off the brake of inertia and attachment, and dive into my clear internal horizons…"

It's so entertaining watching how the wind shape the clouds. It's fun to look for something that I can recognize by its variable shapes. That looks like a winged horse. Next to him there's a flying jockey who also has wings.

What's moving over there? It's a lizard that stays still, looking at me attentively. What might he think of me? "I'm going to touch you without scaring you so that you don't escape and hide. I'll use a trick. I'll touch you with this long and thin stem. I'm slowly moving it closer to you. It's already touching you. You didn't get scared, you're familiar with the stem's touch. It's probably the first time that someone has caressed you this way. You like it, right? You'll be able to tell your grand-children about the adventure you had with the giant forest woman."

The Golden Time

I'm going to live this new day with enchantment. I'm going to wash my eyes, my ears and my mind to perceive what happens inside and outside of me better. I'm not going to move around bewilderedly or be in a hurry. I'm going to calmly enjoy the gifts that life offers me, minute by minute, knowing that with each second that passes, I move forward. I've never thanked Time for inviting me to join in its journey. Why not do it now?

I relax, closing my eyes, breathing calmly. It quietens my mind and inspires me. Let's see what I can tell you:

"Hello, Time, my friend. I really wanted to greet you and thank you for keeping me company. I apologize for hurrying you instead of living, celebrating you... I wanted to tell you that from now on I'm going to wear my ball gown to feel you, savor you, peacefully and without being in a rush.

You know, you mean a lot to me. Thanks to you I'm discovering what a great person I am. I love you and value you a lot more than before. From now on I'm not going to waste you with unnecessary, repetitive, insignificant stories...

I won't wait to celebrate you. I toast in your honor, now! I toast you, me, everyone, Life... more than ever.

I'll take each moment with you as something brand new. I'll use you for the first time, here and now, without missing a single moment of you. I'll breathe you with ecstasy, freedom and sedately without pushing you, without dividing you, without clocks, without giving you an expiry date, without overloading you into my agenda.

You're my biggest gift, Time, my friend. Listen, I've heard that you have a golden time, a time without time, a time outside of time that will allow me to get closer to my Inner Universe and the Universe's Wisdom."

"That's true, Eva. However, I can't give you the golden time, not even the spiritual masters can. Only you have the power to create it, to transmute it, starting from my regularized time. You'll wake it up by practicing meditation. It's the key, the bridge that will drive you to the golden time. You already know it: sitting comfortably with your back straight, you focus your attention on your breathing, you empty your mind, lower it to your inner sky and listen. If you're able to go to that deep silent state, the golden time will come to you, and you'll be in my golden time."

"It sounds easy."

"It seems that way, but it's not. Your thoughts create noise. Your carrousel of daily activities will make it difficult for you to find quiet moments to silence your mind, to give your thoughts a break. If you take a piece of paper and you write down the time that you dedicate to meditating during the day, you might go to bed with a blank sheet of paper. You think that practicing it wastes the time that you need to do your daily, urgent and tangible chores. However, the space that you dedicate to remaining in your heart's golden time is essential for your progress."

The vortex that blew over my life, leaving me without time to sense a flower's smell, a travelling cloud, a child's look of surprise, is becoming history. My attitude, luckily enough, is changing.

What a lovely afternoon! I'm going to move my legs, right here, in this beautiful valley. I'll walk with rhythm, unperturbed, with my hands in my pockets. It seems as though I'm floating, my body is so weightless. It's wonderful to have all the time in the world to waste. It's been a long time since I've whistled! How long? Since I was a child...

It sounds great. I haven't lost any abilities. Wow! I feel so content! This is one of those fantastic moments where everything comes together so that magic, exaltation and ecstasy grow within me. My body takes me as its partner and it uncontrollably drives me to dance. The little birds create the music. I balance myself by holding my arms out like wings and let myself go, allowing my body to choose its movements: I slide around, I jump as light as a ballet dancer, I flutter from one place to another, swaying, moving my winged arms. I can't stop! The dance frenzy has taken over me. My moccasins are like magical slippers that dance and dance and dance untiringly…

Finally, the slippers have pity on me. They smoothly reduce their rhythm and become drowsy. My body rests, lying down weightlessly on Mother Earth.

It's been so indescribable… and it still hasn't ended! I can feel Mother Earth's warm hug, her energy. I'm sure she and the cosmic energies have also given me strength to dance. They've come together to tell me: "Life is beautiful! Don't miss out on anything, and continue using your wings."

"Hi, Eva. An applause. A standing ovation for your dance! It has been a gift for all who have enjoyed it."

"Grandma! I can hear you and I'm not dreaming! I'm wide awake."

"Yes, Eva, you're improving your receptive talents. A fairy has told me she's enjoyed your dance, and she wanted me to thank you because she liked it a lot. She was able to attend thanks to Nature's Deva, who looks after the valley, who told her: "Eva is giving a dance recital. Don't miss it." When you were four years old, one day in the park I asked you if you were speaking to the flower, and you answered, astonished that I couldn't see her, that it was with the fairy with shiny wings next to the flower."

"Grandma, how can I know that it's you, if I can't see you? How can I be sure that you're not a fantasy, an illusion created by my mind or a mocking spirit?"

"That's a very good question Eva, I'm happy you asked. You can't see the presences that communicate with you. You need to be cautious until you know that they have light energies. Energies are like fingerprints. You're good at translating them, you know mine. Whoever the message is from, always consult your heart. It will never deceive you. Within it you have your Inner Master. If a new spirit appears in place of your guides, make sure their energy is light.

When it's a light messenger he always helps you and gives you light, love, peace wisdom... You'll recognize the entities with low energy because the content of their message is inconsistent. Their first communications are normal but they lose quality as time passes. You have to tell them to leave because they're in a light space, because you're light and you don't want them with you. Tell them to go back to the place where they belong.

I gave you the pendant you have hanging from your neck when you were nine years old. On the back of it there's a dedication, which is hardly visible but you know what it says: "To my wonderful princess with a lot of love."

"Yes, that's right, grandma!"

"Later on you'll encounter more tests. We'll keep in touch, Eva. Enjoy your stay in the valley. I love you."

"I love you too, grandma. See you soon."

In the city I would look up, briefly, to look at the stars, captive between buildings, veiled by the street lights. I hardly ever remembered to look at them. The weight of my non-stop chatterbox mind made me stare at the sidewalk practically all the time. It prevented me from realizing that above me there was an infinite sky, full of flashing stellar fireflies waiting to fascinate me with their mystery.

My insatiable cheap ego also intervened. It wouldn't accept competition. It didn't pay attention to them and rejected them. It considered dedicating its attention to looking at a photo where it wasn't the center of attention, as a waste of time. I missed Life's creativity sparks for chasing after the same pointless stickers. I let myself be seduced by the city's commotion, by the groups' whirlwind, their arguments, problems, disqualifications, jealousy...

Paying too much attention to my insignificant and recurring ideas stopped me from seeing things more deeply, from observing a new glow from normal things, surpassing their surface and going into their remarkable depths.

In the city, like in any other place, you can grow spiritually. It's not necessary to isolate yourself in a hermitage or be lost here, surrounded by mountains. During the last months there I had made a good evolutionary leap. In fact, all of the experiences that I've gone through since I was born have made me advance in my life, they've expanded my consciousness.

My personal improvement means having my objectives clear, putting them into action and keeping them focused with fervor, enthusiasm and confidence until I achieve them.

There aren't any mirrors here but I can clearly see my limitations and brightness. I'd never gotten so close to myself. My shadows and lights had never been so exposed.

The city is a good place to learn how to live with other people. This is the perfect place to live with myself, with the squirrels, birds, trees, wind, stars and silence... A silence which is so difficult for me...

What a gigantic tree! It must have been around for so many years. It's like an enormous parasol, its branches touching the ground. It's like a cottage of leaves. The inside is empty, not a single beam from the hot sun enters it. What pleasant surroundings!

"Tree, my friend, I can feel your serene energies in me. I know that you're welcoming me, sensing me. I'm contemplating your radiant aura, your branches' soft splendor and the wonderful show your leaves perform. You're inviting me into an intimate conversation, to communicate with you. Of course I accept, it's a great privilege.

Let me take in some pacifying breaths. They relax me and let my mind descend to my heart so that our dialogue can be more fluid.

Tree, my friend, from my heart now, with my mind still, silent, I am making it more receptive to your thoughts.

You're in love with the breeze. You impatiently wait for it to come, for its caresses to save you from your immobility. You adore it when you feel how it hugs and rocks your branches with tenderness and love. Each and every leaf shudders with emotion, and the magic of the movement moves you. You start a heartfelt dance which is very different to your sluggishness.

Time has filled you with wisdom, tree friend. The rain, which cleanses, has washed away the slag you have gathered over the centuries. So why do you cry sometimes?"

"A lot of my leaves have left me. They've gone, free, with the wind, going to that landscape that everyone talks about. I also dream about flying away to it, but leaving behind my roots..."

"Friend, don't stop now! Go against your comfort zone, attachments and nostalgias that fossilize and isolate you. Fly inside yourself. Live your dreams! You don't have to leave to find that wonderful landscape, it's inside of you! Without moving you can go into it and rock yourself in its horizons for which you yearn so deeply. With your skilled will, focus your mind inwards, toward your heart. Rest it there calmly, silently, and listen. In that magical space you'll find your golden landscape."

"You don't happen to have a pair of swift boots to lend me, do you?"

"That's not the way, dear tree. It means falling and getting up time and again, era after era, drying off your sweat, calming down your exhausted breath, healing your wounds. Step by step until you arrive to the highest point of the watchtower, without hurries and without pauses, not repeating things over and over, erasing old habits, making every day a new day, second by second, being here and now, without letting fear and doubts enter, not darkening or saddening your lift-off by over-doing the same routine. Everyone has their own landscape. This one is yours, designed for you. Enjoy it!

Don't forget to ask. Intensify your desire, shouting loudly: "I want!" It doesn't matter if your voice becomes hoarse or mute. Your mind will pick-up the baton. I want! I want my soul's landscape. I want to arrive to your songs and garlands of flowers, to the center of your universe. Your desire's passion will create the miracle and it will open itself up to you like a flower, offering you its sparkles everywhere, its truths... And each one of your cells, wonderful tree, will whisper to you: "Of course you recognize them. They were already in your heart but you didn't have time to listen to them."

It's an illusion to think that I'm alone. Millions and millions of my friends are always with me. They're my amazing cells. When I jump, they jump with me. When I laugh, they're happy that I'm so content. When I cry they get sad. You do everything that you can to make sure that my body works well. Thank you, each and every one of you. Thank you body, thank you mind, thank you soul, thank you Life, thank you Love, thank you Creator for creating me, for being able to Be.

The little animals of the forest know that I'm here. The stars also know it. My relatives and friends that have crossed to other dimensions are also with me. My Inner Divinity has always been with me, faithful. I'm one of the sparks from the Universe Light. My solitude is an illusion... So much time thinking that I was alone...

I've fallen asleep under this comfortable tree. I'm still sleepy and it's so pleasant. I'm falling asleep again. I have such an easy life... I've heard something that sounded like a voice! Some words, but I could have imagined it, I'm in a drowsy state. There it is again! "Eva, Eva, Eva." I've heard my name at least three times! That gave me goose bumps. "My kingdom for a word"... It's what I said in the valley! "I'm Eva, Eva, Eva, Eva, I'm Eva." I don't get it... It's a parrot! A talking parrot. Ha, ha, ha, ha. It must have heard me complaining in the mountains and it's memorized them. Ha, ha, ha. I didn't specify my request well. I was implying that I wanted to hear human words, not a parrot's. Ha, ha, ha. it's so funny, I can't stop, ha, ha, ha. "Eva, my kingdom, my kingdom." Ha, ha, ha, ha. "No, please, stop already! My stomach hurts from laughing so much."

"Good, talking parrot, welcome to the club. You know you have a home here. I'll continue teaching you more words to increase our dialogue so that you can tell me who has sent you as a messenger."

My hurries are giving in. I have hurried so much during my life. I haven't had time to be fascinated by life, to snoop around, to fall in love with it, to gratefully thank each of my cells for their life, for my life.

I've been a city animal separated from nature, from its harmonizing and peaceful influence. I turned my life into an unstoppable race. It's been an impatient, impulsive marathon, after reaching an "I don't know what," hidden behind my worn-out and insignificant goals, forcing myself to achieve them as soon as possible. Sometimes I wouldn't even start them. That's the way to finish them quickly. Then I'd start other ones right away to be left without free time to find out who I am, to take an inside glimpse at myself.

I've lived by ignoring everything, even if it was thrilling, if it was not in my line of interest. I had the sensation that I was running, without time to lose, chasing after something very important, without knowing what it was, making me classify everything else as a waste of time, that takes me further away from my unknown goal.

The habit of not stopping to observe, contemplate, delve deeper, has made me lose so many gifts, so much emotion, so much fascination, so much life… It's forced me to choose so many mistaken goals. The closer I got to them the further back I went. I ran in the opposite direction of my soul's interests.

Perhaps not knowing how to undo my speed wasn't entirely my fault. We hurry early on in our lives, in the marathon toward the ovum, and after that we don't stop. It could be that the spermatozoids' competitiveness and the pressure to arrive in first position amongst millions of candidates affects our character. Are we born conditioned by a sense of urgency? Nine months waiting to pop out our head and look at life is a respectable amount of time.

Here I have the two main characters responsible for my movie, *The Accelerations*:

The spermatozoid, *applause*, for moving as fast as possible, desperate to reach the goal.

The ovum, *another applause*, waiting without any hurry, sure that with so many million aspirants, one of them will arrive. Interesting, isn't it?

In that exact instant, possibly, inside of me, the two faces that would mark my life defined themselves: hurry and calm, alternately. My hurry, pushed by society or by my tenacious and thirsty insignificances, is usually the winner, although I've discovered a trick for how to beat it: practicing meditation. It hangs up a sign for it: "*The Accelerations* play has been cancelled, there are only tickets for *The Tranquility*, try again in a couple of centuries."

I'm a Universe nomad, a star jumper! Today I'm on this exceptional blue planet, and later on I'll be in other worlds that will surprise me with even more of the Creator's marvels. Why, then, am I so accelerated? Well, finally, I'm able to reduce my hurries a bit, my accelerations…

Okay, I'll be faithful with this argument. I'll take a pause. I'll close my eyes and enjoy listening to the beautiful sounds in this kingdom of nature in which I'm immersed.

Oh no, the door of the shelter is open. I left in such a hurry that I forgot the closing command. What's that noise in the kitchen?! It sounds like a bear's claws scratching the refrigerator! Could I have left it open and now the bear is eating up the supplies? I'll get the shepherd's cane. It's in the kitchen! I'll climb up a tree. Do bears climb up trees? I think they do. I'll go inside the bathroom, I'll close the door and I'll wait until it leaves. It's leaving! I can see its foot... What!? It's the squirrel!

"Man, you scared me to death! I confused you for a bear's foot. Wow! You've eaten all of my hazelnuts. You've gobbled them all up shamelessly. Look at what a big gut you've got now! It almost touches the ground. You know what, you've furtively sneaked in. What you've done isn't okay. One thing is to come and visit me and another is to come and empty the pantry. Don't pretend you can't hear me."

The Four Pyramids

I'll water the daisies. "You're so beautiful". What's this tip doing inside the flowerpot's soil? A tiny quartz-glass pyramid! What does it remind me of? Here's another one. The daisies were covering them. They're identical. Now I remember! They're the same ones that my warrior gave me during my dream. I counted four. I'll look for the other ones... I'm so gullible, it was only a coincidence... another one! And the fourth one! There aren't anymore. It's more than a coincidence. They're identical.

They're so beautiful. The Sun hits them entirely and stunning reflections are projected onto the table! I know they have a message for me, on behalf of my warrior but they don't have anything engraved. The four of them are the same. I'll keep on looking at them to see if I get the message. Maybe it's in their reflection of the sun. I don't know how to receive it. I'll meditate. Let's see if it comes to me. I close my eyes, take in some pacifying breaths... They're so pleasant.

I love being in this peaceful state. How much time has passed by? Oh, the pyramids! I almost forgot them with my meditation. Their message... I've got it! The pyramids' shadows form a three-letter word on the table. Two pyramids overlapping or touching each other form the letter M, and the other two, separated, individually create the letter A. If I place them one after another, they construct the word AMA, which translated means "love". It's a fantastic message, my warrior's banner.

I have a cold. My nose is like a fountain and I just can't stop sneezing. It's not surprising with these abrupt weather changes. I'll use this time to practice what I've read in the book that deals with how to heal illnesses with love. Let's see how it goes:

I'm aware that this cold is a way to heal and purify my body, which will help me eliminate toxins.

I don't fight against it. I accept it as a teacher that visits me during a period of time to help me become healthy, and give me lessons of patience, tolerance, humility... I don't label it as being bad luck, an annoying problem, but as a situation that gives me personal advancement, a stimulus.

I'll take in some healing breaths with the intention and trust that they'll heal my cold. I straighten out my back, get comfortable, relax. I quiet my mind, breathing in through my nose, imagining, visualizing a bright ray of the Universe's energy descending over my head, flowing through my column to my solar plexus. Exhaling, I spread the energy to each and every one of my cells, organs, to my entire body, filling, bathing them, with its healing, invigorating light, full of love energy. Or I can instruct it to go where it's needed. I beg you, Inner Wisdom, to help me throughout this process.

There are so many fallen trees. They've been demolished by the wind's fury, the powerful lightning and the impact of the big rocks that have fallen from the mountains. The erosion of the elements has deprived them of their bark, giving them an extremely bare appearance.

They look like shipwrecks, destroyed when they crashed into the rocks, pushed by the wave's fury. There's a multitude of broken trunks and branches everywhere. They look like mammoth and dinosaur skeletons. Their whitish color reminds me of an elephant cemetery on a steppe covered by snow. They create a prehistoric-like landscape full of desolation. The high mountains impoverish the light, painting the scenery in gray, which increases the somber and depressing feeling of this bewitching place. It seems as though time has stopped here.

This area is suggestive but it's discouraging me. I'll go to the volcano lake and have a bath. If I'm lucky, I'll meet up with my friends there, the monkey family.

You can breathe so much peace in this place. I'll sit down in lotus posture because if I lie down I'll fall asleep. Back straight, I breathe through my nose, relaxingly. It's great to feel the fresh air enter my lungs, inhaling and exhaling softly. It's such a joy! I feel so peaceful. Every time I find my breathing more delightful.

It's the right time to pause for a moment and reflect on this morning's reading. It was very interesting. The author talks about emotional and intuitive states and mental and rational ones. I'm going to think about it. Let's see what I can come up with. I'll take the essential parts of the topic and develop it my way. I hope the word juice I create tastes good.

It doesn't mean carrying a full bag on my back, far from my heart, packed with rancid, false, numbered, predetermined emotions. It doesn't mean emptying them all of a sudden with gestures, excitement and confusion, when I meet up with somebody, as if it were a TV contest with an entertaining public that has been instructed and has rehearsed what they have to do. However, I can't be the other extreme: taking on the impenetrable expression of a card player, controlling my emotions, making my feelings cold and hiding them with a mask that doesn't give a glimpse of any emotional change, because one day, as a result of hiding them so much, when I look for them, I won't find them. They'll have left me.

If what I think, say or do comes from my heart's love, my thoughts, words and actions will be crystalline, beautiful and positive. Love transforms everything that comes out of me into something luminous.

The children let their euphoric emotions loose. They don't hide them behind an unfazed face because they don't think that they can be impure, inappropriate, out of order or seen as infantile. They feel their emotions and, without anything else, they let them fly like doves in the sky. They openly look at things. Their eyes stick to whatever astonishes them, with an expression of delight on their faces.

It's the excited emotion inside of me that breaks the molds of what's discolored and opens up the doors to *my prodigious changes*, to my life's magic. I can see clearly now. I'll go into my heart and I'll make sure that there isn't anything that might hinder my feelings from flowing.

This certainly isn't a good place to reflect. All of the parrots sing at the same time. What a deafening serenade! It sounds like they're sawing something. How do they understand each other? It's full of flies that don't stop landing on me. I brush them off. They swarm around and come back again. I have three options: let them walk freely all over my body, fan them away continuously, which is annoying, or look for another place. I'm going to explore...

Oooh! What a surprise! I can't believe it. I've finally found it. There's the flagstone walkway that will guide me to *The Rock from the Past*. I'll walk faster...

Once again, I'm on the rock. My heart is beating so fast. I'm really impatient to know more about my past life. I'm going into a trance, receiving images. Eras are coming together. I'm in her time, her circumstances. I can see her sitting down, pensive. She's in her small cell. I am in communion with her, with myself. She's me. We're one. Our immortal spirit. I'm receiving her thoughts:

I still don't like the Residence. It's a very old, somber, dismal, humid, dark construction. The windows are narrow openings that light can hardly pass through. During its long history it's been used as a fortress, a temple, a monastery... They've been restoring it. They've transformed it into the community's residence.

When the important people of the community discovered that I had the ability to communicate messages from other spaces, they asked my parent's permission to intern me in the Residence. The reason, according to them, was to preserve and enhance my talents. Initially, my parents didn't allow it. With time they convinced them and they interned me. I went from being in fields full of sun and flowers to the somber darkness of the Residence. I changed from being a small, trotting gazelle to an imprisoned bird in its cage, deprived of its song.

The moment I went through the thick entrance hall door I felt isolated, imprisoned. My parents and friends' warm and vibrant love was substituted by the cold severity of the residents. It put an end to my freedom. Being separated from what I loved the most in the world made a repulsion grow within my heart toward my talent. I could hear my friends' shouts of joy through the Residence's thick walls. Hearing them hum, play, fight, scream... broke my heart. Birds have a time for their songs and for their silences. They don't put a plug on their joy of life. They demonstrate it, pouring it out. The residents ended my singing. They left me only with silence.

I didn't understand why I was cruelly locked up, isolated from the outside world, because from the outside I was also able to receive and transmit the voices.

They didn't worry about giving explanations, and even less to a little girl. It was like putting me in prison. I rebelled against the unjust decision, but it was in vain.

The resident's discipline slowly saddened the happy, playful little girl that I was. They stole my childhood. They isolated me. They treated me like an adult, with the same silence and contemplation exercises, and their strict eating habits.

For them, I represented the possibility of hearing the teachings of the masters. They subjected me to an exaggerated protection that embittered my existence. My pain and rejection to this very unjust situation almost ruined my talent.

I spent most of my time crying, missing my loved ones. I locked myself in, keeping myself to myself... like them. The

Residence's darkness put an end to my enjoyment of Life. I wasn't able to overcome it. I could have done the same work without being interned.

The masters must be really disappointed with our slow progress. They have a lot of patience with our delay in assimilating their teachings. They send us their messages full of love to soften our hard shells formed by archaic habits and beliefs, but it's difficult for us. They repeat the same messages to us, in a very beautiful way, year after year, so that they can soak us, helping us to develop our consciousness.

It's difficult for us to change, to incorporate their teachings. They frequently remind us of how important it is that we practice quieting our mind, keeping it silent to expand our consciousness, so that Life can give it the ideas that we need. They tell us what we are lacking and we try to overcome it, but it's so difficult to change our embedded habits. They have so much strength!

I'm aware that my censorship and dislike toward the residents is influenced by my bitterness at having been confined by them in the Residence. Not getting along with them doesn't allow me to judge them impartially. I'm too hard on them and I look at their shadows, instead of their qualities. I need to control my judgmental tendency.

I know that they want to learn, to integrate the messages' teachings, and that they fight to get rid of their old habits. However, habits are hard to change, and they make it difficult for them to assimilate the lessons.

They arrived here when they found out about the voices, from different origins, which sometimes causes tension among them, due to their different lifestyles. However, their desire and fervor to follow the teachings makes those tensions diminish.

Their austerity, their silence and their seriousness inhibit me. Maybe they think that life's joy, happiness and a good sense of humor are opposed to spiritual advancement.

The flow of images has been cut off. My mind's screen is now empty. Now I know why in my present life I never wanted to know anything about paranormal phenomena nor be in closed spaces. Communicating the masters' messages ruined my childhood. It forced me to be separated from my environment and loved ones. The past is returning again... The images and thoughts are coming back...

The voices trust me. I can't say no to transmitting them. Without me, their messages wouldn't be received by the community. I'm aware that I'm lending a service of great value to those who listen to them. The masters' teachings are expanding their consciousness, their love, their light...

At the beginning, the residents were suspicious of me, but when they saw that I was a transmitter with few personal influences, and that I faithfully transferred the voices' messages, they began to trust me and also the masters.

Their messages are very useful. They frequently underline the great importance of keeping our mind silent in order to expand our consciousness. They also tell us how we can get better crops, or issues about health, living with other people... They send us messages to balance out the rights between men and women, in a community where men are the ones who distribute the bread. They tell us that happiness and humor are important to advance our spiritual path. They warn us in advance of when hordes, that from time to time devastate the territory, will arrive. This way we can save ourselves. The masters show us their naturalness and humility when they tell us that they also continue learning.

The Scribe

She's still in the penumbra of her tiny cell, lost in thought, looking far away through the small window. I'm receiving her thoughts:

I'm becoming the same as them, quiet, distant, serious... I don't have anyone to communicate with, or be sincere to, only myself. I still don't fit in here. The people here feel comfortable with seriousness and monotony. I still feel delight, creativity and joy. They like silence, that silence that I find so full of reproach. They think that they need it for their spiritual development, and yes, it is necessary but they should alternate it with understanding, smiles, happiness, naturalness, tolerance, will to live, words...

However, my despair has been declining. Over time, I've discovered the benefit that staying at the Residence has had. The masters fill me with their peaceful, loving energy during the dictations. Now I consider my talent a privilege, instead of misfortune, as I had previously qualified it.

The transmissions are like recesses inside the gray, sad world of the Residence. The messages' transcription fills me with love and peace. It helps me resist my sadness and solitude. It intensifies the languid flame, which my life has turned into. Sometimes I can see how the masters' bright light descends over us, increasing our brilliance.

Lowering my mind to my heart, free of thoughts, substitutes the cloister's darkness for my inner brilliant states. It also helps to strengthen my mind and alleviate my sad states.

I'm proud of my work. It's necessary to ensure the messages get through to those who come to hear them. I'm aware that my labor is for the good of the community. The teachings improve their consciousness and mine too. The masters' dictations have benefited me, enriching my attitude toward life and they've improved my capacity to love, my understanding of life and death.

I'm waiting impatiently to return to the message rock. Being on top of it, feeling the wind's strength, the master's loving energy and the community's devotion. I feel useful. The master has told us that the transmissions are also heard by beings of other dimensions.

Now, looking back, I know that I judged the residents harshly. I made mistakes in some of my judgments. I demanded that they be perfect and, like everyone, they have limitations. They have different personalities, sometimes opposite. What brings them together is their search for truths. Now I know that some of their decisions and attitudes have helped me develop.

I was a great treasure to them. Thanks to my help, they were able to receive the masters' precious teachings. That's why they isolated me, so that they could protect me against accidents, make me healthier by controlling my diet, and nurture and increase my talent.

I didn't realize it then. I saw them with my child-like mind, like bad ogres in a fairytale. However, they should have combined their mind's silent reasoning with their heart's cheerful emotion. Everyone is different. Now I accept them for who they are, paying attention to their qualities rather than focussing on their defects.

The images have disappeared. I've lost contact... It's coming back! The album, from which my soul continues to reveal memories from one of my past lives, reappears.

A young man in the Residence! He and two residents are coming toward me. He's tall and thin, wearing a plain cloth tunic. He greets me by tilting his head forward. He looks at me intensely. Something new is born inside of me... His presence makes the resident's voice seem distant, turned off: "And from now on the scribe will be with you, with writing tablets prepared to note down all of the voices' messages the moment they reach you."

His presence revives me strongly. His arrival has awakened my desire to live and the sun shines again in my heart. He was also confined in a community during his youth because of his talent as a scribe.

In front of the residents we didn't look at each other, or we did it furtively, so that they wouldn't perceive our great love, separate us, and expel him from the temple. My love sits down next to his table, placing his writing tools on it, and I sit down on the rug with my legs crossed. That's how we wait, immobile, mute, with our eyes closed, sending and receiving our love's energy, until the voices appear. This is how we can be together without causing suspicion.

At the beginning, from time to time, we strongly felt the desire to run off, leave, escape. We resisted because we knew that we would leave the entire community without the messages' teachings. I also sensed that we had made a pact to do this mission together, before we were born, when we were preparing for our work on Earth for this incarnation. This is why my love and I are still here.

Who's shouting? The residents are in the patio surrounding a man that I don't know. Who could he be? He's tall, robust and looks jovial. He has a clear, powerful and sonorous voice and a strong personality. He doesn't hide his emotions, nor does he lower his voice tone like the residents who speak in near whispers. They treat him attentively. Often his laughter explodes into a spurt of joy. It's so strange, laughter in the Residence, so nice! It's been a long time since I've heard laughter's rejuvenating sound.

He's seen me. He apologizes by saying: "Forgive me brothers." He's coming toward me! He's left them speechless. They try to control themselves, but you can tell how annoyed they are. What could he want? He looks so welcoming and he has such a big and honest smile.

"Hello, you must be the Residence's little transmitter. You've become a beautiful woman. I've heard a lot about you and your wonderful transmitting abilities. I'm Cir, the Residence's architect. I really wanted to meet you. I know that with your talent you're helping the community grow. I want to thank you for the great service that you've given with your messages. I know that you've paid a lot for it, with your childhood and a big part of your freedom. That's why I've brought you a gift, so that you can share it with the scribe. It's going to fill you both with joy. Yes, I know about your great love. Don't be afraid. For a long time I was in charge of restoring the Residence. I fell passionately in love with a wonderful woman who was also interned and, like you, we had to keep it a secret."

"Cir, I'm also glad I've met you. I know, because of the problems you went through, that you understand our situation. I appreciate your discretion. Can you tell me what your gift is?"

"Of course. As the Residence's architect, I was able to create a wonderful place for my love and I, impossible to be discovered by the residents. I offer it to you with my friendship, if you want it, it's yours."

"What an unexpected gift! We accept and thank you for your generosity."

"It's a privilege to be able to help you. Let me know when you want me to show you how to get there."

"Thank you, Cir, for coming into our lives. I'm so emotional. It's because I'm so thankful to you. We'll always keep you in our hearts.

"I'll always remember you, too. You're beings with a lot of light. I have another gift. You don't have to worry anymore if the residents find out about your love."

"It would be a big relief, but it's impossible. They're very strict about this issue."

"You're mistaken. They've known about your relationship since the beginning. They were the ones who encouraged it."

"They encouraged it! I can't believe it! I don't understand. Why did they do it?

"They realized that you and your talent were languishing. Your emotional state continued to deteriorate, you became sick and you stopped transmitting. They recognized their mistake, isolating you, instead of doing good to you, it was eliminating your power. They thought that if you had someone young beside you it would revive you, you would be reborn and transmit the voices again. They put aside their prejudices because the most important thing was to continue receiving the messages. And that's how it happened. They were right about their decision. They introduced you to the young scribe."

"Cir, your words are really confusing me. I would never have imagined it."

"They were certain. They could either consent your love or lose the masters' messages. They decided to continue receiving them."

"It was a blessing to lose my talent because it helped them make that decision. More than once, my love and I thought about leaving the Residence and going somewhere far away from here, but not being able to give the community the voices' teachings stopped us. We were going to propose to continue to give them the messages, just like always, living outside of the Residence, without hiding our love. From what you just revealed to me, I think it's very likely that they'll accept. What do you think, Cir?"

"Well I already discussed it with them. I've told them that it would favor the messages' flow, and they've agreed."

"That's wonderful news! I'm so happy!"

"They've asked me to be the middleman and to plan the date when you'll leave. Meanwhile, you can discreetly use the place that I've given to you. What do you think?"

"Cir, thank you so much for what you're doing for us. You've brought a fresh and pure breeze to the Residence. You don't keep your emotions locked up like the residents do. It's difficult to deal with their reserved, absent minded personalities."

"They have good hearts and they're making an effort to brighten-up their light. When they heard that there was a girl here that transmits the truths from the masters in other dimensions, their hearts lit up and they got moving, without worrying about the hardships or how long they had to travel to get here. Over the years they've come together from different places, even though the differences in their personal stories sometimes cause them problems."

They have different ideas and beliefs. Each one of them bears layers of old habits, accumulated in the places they've lived. It's difficult for them to get rid of them, but they're making an effort. The search for the truth is what brings them together, the desire to expand their knowledge, their love.

They know that each of them has their own place on the path, moving ahead at a different pace. The important thing is that they feel the impulse to continue to move forward, because they know that they're eternal and that they'll all reach the Light. The masters' transmissions are bringing them together, smoothing out their tensions, their differences. They find it difficult to wake them up, but they're very patient and they love them unconditionally.

My way of being makes them somewhat uncomfortable because it reflects some of their differences. It shakes up their habits, deflates their egos and shows them that happiness doesn't conflict with spiritual progression, but that it actually helps it.

I used to lower my tone, my enthusiasm and creativity so that they wouldn't feel uncomfortable. The day came when I decided to be myself. Now I behave just as I am. I suppose Life uses me as a tool to forge its changes.

The retrospective images leave. Time's screen disconnects... No, they're coming back again... She... I... I'm part of a circle with the residents. We're standing, silently. In the middle of it there's a man holding a crystal with both hands. It's Cir, the crystal guardian. He moves slowly, with his eyes closed in order to concentrate better on our energy flow, coming and going, frequently changing directions. He stands still, turns around, and walks toward me. He stands in front of the person on my left. It looks like he's made his decision. No, he steps to the side and stands in front of me! He keeps his eyes closed. I hold my breath…

A lot of time is passing by. It seems endless to me. He opens his eyes. They look at mine. My tears start to flow uncontrollably. Cir hands me the crystal. I take it carefully. You can tell by the residents' faces that they're shocked. They didn't expect that a woman would be the receiver and guardian of the crystal, the highest privilege that someone can receive in the community.

The entire community has gathered at the square to hear the master's urgent message. I'm receiving his energy, I begin to transcribe. "This is a farewell message, but you'll continue to receive our voices at more subtle internal levels. Difficult times are approaching. It's a very crucial moment in your lives. You've been developing during these years, faithfully following the teachings. Contemplation, reflection and mental tranquility exercices have helped you improve your consciousness. You know that a life is like a blink of an eye in your eternal existence. You're ready to confront situations that others might find difficult, even accepting your transition with peace in your hearts and a smile on your lips.

Some barbarian hordes are getting close. They were heading south, but, unexpectedly, they've changed their trajectory and they're coming towards here with the intention of exterminating you, destroying everything and using the Residence as their main base. There are a lot of them, trained for battle. They're well armed and their horses are fast. Wherever they go they leave death and destruction. You wouldn't even survive their first attack.

Maybe some of you will leave your earthly body today. It's a change of dimension. You're ready. You'll take with you all the improvements that you've made during this life, because they are not materialistic. They're subtle states of the soul and developments of the spirit. The crystal we've entrusted to you, which you've taken care of up to now, will have to remain dormant until you recover it again, when the golden era arrives. The bearer of the legacy will be guided to the place where it will be kept.

You have to leave immediately. Don't waste time taking anything with you. You're already taking the most important thing with you, your life. Leave and scatter. Mix with different people and, using your way of life as an example, spread the light, love and peace teachings that you've been receiving. Be guiding lights for others. Remember that you've come to awaken people's consciousness.

As eras pass by, you'll find each other again in the time of the prodigies. You won't recognize each other. You will have forgotten. You'll come together because of the stars' legacy mission. Go now, quickly. They're very close. Light, love and peace."

We don't have time to waste. The women, children, elderly and married men can flee using the river. Take the boats. The current is very fast and will take you far. They won't be able to reach you as the land next to the river is very rocky and will slow down the horses. Don't light bonfires until you're out of danger. Follow the escape plan.

Single men, take the horses. Your mission is to protect the legacy. Leave false tracks. There are many of them and they're well armed. Do everything you can to slow them down so that the crystal guardian, guided by the voices, can arrive to the place where the stars' legacy will be protected...

"We'll wait for them here. They have to pass by this narrow-path. It's very difficult and sharp. "Yes, we'll cut them off." "And from up here we'll have an advantage." "We'll attack by surprising them and hit them with a load of rocks and arrows." "Don't worry, we'll stop them here." "Not even one will pass through us. We'll detain them so that you can flee."

"Three come with me, so that we can protect the oracle. May the Supreme Creator protect you."

"And you too, brothers."

My opinion about the residents has changed. I haven't heard a single complaint from them. They've all volunteered, without any objections, to protect the stars' legacy. They're all courageously willing to die in the canyon. I used to judge them blindly, but those days are over. When we said goodbye, I saw a glow of appreciation and admiration in their eyes. My tears showed them how much I love them. Our past problems and insignificances have disappeared completely.

"They weren't able to stop all of them. Some were able to cross the canyon. Here come the first five who have made it. The ones who still haven't succumbed are probably fighting with all of their might so that the rest of them don't cross. They're probably having a difficult time. There are just too many of them."

"The one with the spotted horse looks like the boss. If he falls, maybe the other ones will flee."

There are so many arrows! They're also aiming at the horses. They've hit mine! They've knocked me down. I'm running out of arrows!

"They're beating us! Let's take cover behind the trees. I've hit one of them."

"All of our men are dead. I've hit another one. Only the one with the spotted horse is left. He's aiming at you. I'll cover you, my love."

"Don't protect me. No! He's hit you with another arrow."

"I've run out of arrows. I'll throw a knife at him. I've missed. Ahhh! He's hit me with another arrow."

"He's slowly preparing another arrow. He knows that we can't defend ourselves and that we're under his control. We're in big trouble. Supreme Creator, help us."

"Flee so that you can guard the crystal."

"His horse got scared, it saw a snake. It stands up and moves back on its hind legs, tripping over a fallen trunk, losing its balance, and collapsing. The rider flies off. He falls roughly, hitting himself against a rock. He's absolutely still. I feel a lacerating desperation within me. I can feel the three arrows that are piercing your chest.

My love, why did you stand in front of me when the arrows were directed at me?"

"Because you are my life."

"My love, don't leave! Don't leave me alone."

"Don't cry, be strong. You know that we'll find each other again, we were and we will eternally be one."

"Yes, I know, but I have you so deeply within me. I love you so much. The pain breaks my heart, it's so difficult to leave you. I can't abandon you. It's stronger than me."

"You're not leaving me. My spirit is always intact. It doesn't die, it only changes dimension. It will continue contacting your spirit. Our souls will continue to find each other during the course of time, loving each other on Earth and in Heaven, our love will last forever. In less than a butterfly's flutter we'll be together again in another life, in the golden era."

"I'm okay now, I don't want to ruin your rebirth in the new space. I am at peace with saying goodbye to you, knowing that our spirits will stay in touch, without the borders of time and space."

"Now, I can see the light of my guides. I can feel their love. My spirit is starting to leave my body. This end is a beginning, death is a birth."

"Yes, that's the way it works. Thank you my love, for your hopeful and strong words. I can see your guides. It's comforting to see how they pass their love energies and light to you. They beg me not to hold you back, but that I should help them facilitate your spirit's departure to that other level. They're telling me that you can leave now. It's easy for you because you're not holding on to life, your spirit has almost left your body. You can also help by letting yourself go... Okay, my love, you have freed yourself from your body. Your spirit has departed completely, gently. They're receiving you, welcoming you. I can hear your thoughts."

"I'm happy here, meeting my light family again. I'm extremely content to see that you're all right. I love you. Remember we have a date during the time of the prodigies."

"I have it engraved in my heart, my love."

"More barbarians are coming. I can see the cloud of dust made by their horses. Save the crystal, you don't have a lot of time. Run and hide it. If they catch you they'll kill you and they'll take the legacy. Our friends' deaths and ours will have been in vain."

"Yes, my love. Be happy. I love you."

The Stars' Legacy

I'm receiving the master's energy.

"Master. Where to? How much longer will it be?"

"We're here. Go toward the trees. The entrance is behind those tangled bushes. Go between the ones with red berries."

"There's a rocky wall in front of me that's stopping me. What should I do?"

"Get close to it. Take a step forward. Put your hand on the 'Om' sign that's engraved on the rock. Yes, that one. It will recognize your vibration and open the heavy flagstone."

"All right. It's opening."

"It will close itself. To get out put your hand over the 'Om' sign, located on the other side of the door."

"Okay, it's starting to close."

"The people who are chasing you haven't seen you enter. The flagstone camouflages itself perfectly with the rocky wall. They'll get tired of looking for you and they'll leave confused. You'll be able to leave safely tomorrow. Put the crystal inside the chest located in the niche. It will wait for the new era there. You'll be in charge of rescuing it. Until then, you won't hear my words like you're hearing them now. You'll be able to catch glimpses of them in your heart. You're moving very well along this incarnation's road. Don't worry about asking me for anything you might need. I'll receive your plea at any time."

"Dear master, I can't hold back my tears, my deep sadness. I have lost the two beings I've loved the most in my life: my love and you."

"You never lose anyone. We all continue. They're stages. One finishes and another one begins. In a tiny amount of time, you'll be together physically, navigating on Earth. Don't attach yourself to things. It's important to know how to let them go. Life's tide will join you again in the appropriate moment. Spiritually we always fly together. Remember that Life always helps you. Light, love and peace."

"Thank you, master. I'll always keep you in my heart."

I leave the crystal, automatically, where the master has told me. I drop to my knees, collapse, curl up and cry uncontrollably. I'm receiving my love's thoughts. I react. I get up. I stop crying. I don't want to sadden him with my pain. The feeling of being apart is an illusion. I can feel him next to me. Our spirits will continue to meet each other in matter. I know that our love will continue through space and time.

You'll rest here, stars' legacy. Thanks to a brave group I've been able to keep you safe, waiting for the time, the Golden Era, in which we humans will have expanded our consciousness, making it possible to receive you.

Tomorrow I'll head out and look for the others. Maybe we'll find each other in another place. My love and the master will guide me and protect me. I'll continue to spread the teachings...

The image is fading. I've lost it. Time has balanced itself toward here and now. Once again I'm on the rock, moved with nostalgia and anguish because of what I've been through. It's all been so implausible. My knowledge from my last life will influence my current decisions a lot.

The splendid beauty that surrounds me is stimulating my artistic talent. I used to pass by it without seeing it, and now I'm fascinated by all its details: a pebble, a tree's bark, the lichen on a rock... It's likely that meditating is improving my senses, my perception and my observation capacity.

It's a shame that I don't have a camera to take photos of so much creativity. It would be better to capture them with my eyes and file them in my heart.

This flat area full of rocks is like an immense exhibition of outdoor sculptures. A sculptor would have a marvelous time here. Most of them seem abstract and the others remind me of realistic things. The lichens, little flowers, moss, roots that cover them combine well with the rock's color, its texture, their fissures, their grains' tone…

The rocks are also vulnerable. The roots of the trees and plants break through their cracks and as they grow, the rock breaks. Even something as inconsistent as the water goes through its fissures and, when it freezes, it cracks them. The rock must be surprised when it sees how a little root or the inoffensive water has the power to break it.

During millions of years the rocks from the high mountains have been falling off. Some of them have landed in the river bed. The rain, the wind and the river's current have eroded, polished, filed their edges, rounded their corners, covering their haughtiness and arrogance with a mantel of humility, until they have transformed the gigantic rocks into simple oval pebbles of whitish color, settled on the river's bed. The bigger ones look like dinosaur eggs.

With a little more time, a thousand or million years more, I don't know, this pebble will have transformed itself into a tiny grain of sand that will contain all its history, the essence of when it was a gigantic rock. Nature is such a good teacher. It's nice to stop and read her.

I also, with time and Life's current, will file my thorns, rounding, illuminating my spirit, just like the Universe's bubbles: the Sun, the Earth, the moon, the stars…

This rocky wall is so familiar yet there's nothing special about it. My vibration is increasing. I can feel an energy that's stronger on the right side, still increasing… There's an Om sign engraved on the rock. I'm in front of the cave where I hid the crystal during one of my past lives! I'm trembling so much.

Destiny has brought me to the same place, after jumping in time. What for? It's obvious. They told me a long time ago. "When the time of the prodigies arrives you'll recover the crystal legacy."

I'm going to put my hand over the "Om" sign. It surprisingly reminds me of an "E", the first letter in my name. My hand is shaking a lot. I'm hesitant, I don't dare. On one, two, three... Go! It's already on to it, the system is similar to the shelter's opening. I can sense a vibration. The rock door is opening up! Smoothly, even though it weighs so much. I have chills! Now I can enter… It closes on its own, like in the past…

The walls emit the same soft white phosphorescence as in the shelter, illuminating the entire cave. They're covered with very artistic curved signs. They look like they're dancing.

There's the chest where I put the crystal! I've got goose bumps. No-one has been here since then. It's so exciting. It has been waiting for so many centuries for me to arrive and recover it.

It's clear that the reason I'm in these desert mountains is to recover the crystal. What do I have to do with it? I don't have the connection with the master's voice in this life, which used to guide me back then. He might come back to give me some clues.

What's that noise, that racket? It's a landslide! I have to leave immediately. Aah! A big rock has hit my leg. It's so painful. I think it's broken. There's such a gigantic dust cloud, I can hardly see. What an intense pain! Thank goodness! The landslide has stopped. The rock has trapped my leg! I can't free it…

I've always had a certain respect for death, and now that I feel that I'm going to leave, I'm at peace, calm and full of confidence. I neither have fear nor feeling of failure or punishment, I see it as a change, a trip, like a door that separates one room from the other, like a vacation after the school year, to restore my strength. I know it's the way to freedom and peace. My life will continue in another space. I have more time, more lives in front of me. My spirit's adventure doesn't end here, it continues and continues. I'm eternal.

However, I'd like to continue living so that I can complete the crystal legacy mission and focus my life in another way, without planning so much. Living more in the present. Enjoying it with love, tolerance, understanding, illusion and with the joy of living. Forgiving myself and others. Stopping to savor the small details. Letting myself be driven by my feelings. Airing my intuition. Singing to life as if I were a nightingale, without hoping to be front page news. With a smile of joy for what I have, instead of a suffering frown for what I lack. Amending everything that has stopped me from living to the fullest. I know that this fervent recognition of how I would have liked to have been in the past and the burning and passionate desire to have achieved it could make the miracle happen: that I will integrate this right now as I depart, making it part of my stellar backpack, of my eternal light baggage.

I can see, from far away, the most important events in my life pass by, quickly, fleeting.

So much wasted time and resources spent wandering away from the meaning of life, dramatizing petty things, insignificant questions, instead of easing them with a smile and a good sense of humor.

I could have done it better. I lived so much of my life poorly, superficially, focusing on fashionable goals, ignoring everything that had nothing to do with them, that life wisely offered me. I suffocated the good moments because of: "What will they say?" "It's a waste of time." "It won't turnout okay." "What will I gain from it?" "My name doesn't appear in big letters, it's not first."

In my future lives I'll do better. During this one there's been all types of situations that, without me realising it, have made me grow to a higher or lesser degree. During these last few months, I've advanced, I've been smart enough to do some cleaning, and

I've woken up, started things that were struggling to get out of my heart. I've gathered a lot of lights, invisible advances made by my soul. I have them forever in my backpack of stars. They'll come with me to my new home, throughout my existence.

I'll have more lives, more upgrades, with better benefits, more advances to improve my program: *I, Eva, searching for the Light.* I have all the time in the world to perfect it, no more or less than eternity.

However, Creator, I beg you for an extension. Grant me some more time. It's not because I'm afraid of the transit, it's because I haven't finished developing my consciousness. My mind and heart are reviving. Now that, finally, I feel okay on this blue planet, passionately in love with life, you give me the boarding card. Yes, I know. I chose it.

I'm enjoying everything so much. I'm going through a good patch with my inner development and I'm on my honeymoon with myself, with Life. It was difficult to reconcile with her, with me, with You. I'm changing so many things about myself, progressing, recognizing who I am, filling my stellar backpack with sparks of light, improvements... I beg You, if it's possible, to delay my departure. However, You know what's best for me.

I'm aware that everything You've brought and everything You'll bring to my life, to my existence, is what's best for my growth. I know that I chose it in the ambitious work plan that I chose for this life before being born. Maybe I also contemplated the possibility of begging you for this extension. Please can You move the counters in my life's game?

I understand and accept that life is a game that I've received to learn from, to improve and surpass myself. Like all games it has a beginning and an end. While it lasts all types of things happen, excellent, good and not so good. It's an adventure with its ups and downs: illnesses, joys, failures, achievements, fears, setbacks... They're all counters that belong to the didactic game of life. They've all helped me to grow, to forge my strength, my will, my love, my consciousness, to brighten up my heart, my light...

If You don't grant me the extension, if I have to leave, maybe it'll be because I've completed my mission on this blue planet, the mission that I chose before I was born, and because I've already received my diploma for my studies. Maybe it's not time to rescue the crystal yet, maybe the plan has been postponed. It will be given in another incarnation. Perhaps the conditions are still not the correct ones...

I feel tides of pain. I'm fainting. I can't handle this situation. "I beg You to take control. You know which direction is best for me. I only know a few answers in this wonderful and endless adventure that is my existence. I hand over the control to You." My grandmother's prayer has popped into my mind: Lord, do Your will in me. "Thank you, grandma, it comforts me. Lord, do Your will in me."

Where am I? Ah, I'm in the cave! I haven't died! I don't dare open my eyes, I am afraid of seeing my leg destroyed. I heard the bone when it fractured. I don't feel any pain! It's not caught by the rock! Where's the rock? It's that one. How did it get over there? Not even a group of men could have moved it. Maybe the master, the light team of the crystal's mission, my grandma, my guides... instruments of the Creator's, have taken out their magic wand and gently lifted it so as not to injure me, and moved to the other side.

I'm moving it! I can move my leg! I'm going to get up. Great, my legs can handle my weight. They can keep me up. My broken bone is fixed! My pants are destroyed, but my leg shows no signs of an injury. I can walk perfectly. The pain is gone.

What's that loud sound? Another landslide! Go toward the door, quick, quicker, I forgot the crystal! It's too far away. I won't get there on time and I'll get trapped again.

My love and the others gave up their lives to protect it! Here I go. Faster. There's so much racket! I can hardly see through the dust. I have it! Go toward the exit at full speed. I'm here. My hand is over the opening sensor. Oh no, it won't open! Come on, come on, open up. Don't fail me now. What a big dust cloud! Rock splinters are falling close to me. Yes, yes, it's opening up! I run as fast as my legs can carry me. I run in the other direction, protecting myself from the river of rocks that are falling outside.

The entrance has been sealed by tons of rocks. What tension! It's daytime. It's so nice to feel the breeze. I'm going to relax by taking in a few deep breaths. The crystal is creating iridescent gleams with the sunbeams. It's so beautiful… "Thank you, Creator, for the extension, for giving me more time." An energy, a voice, is entering my mind. I've heard it before. "Who are you?"

"Time's magic brings us together again."

"Master! It's been such a long time since I've channeled your teachings to the community, announcing an era full of love and peace to them."

"Yes, Eva, that leap in time is occurring now, we're entering it."

"Can you show me more of my mission's counters?"

"Let time flow. You'll discover them on your own at the correct moment. Life will place them in front of you as your consciousness learns to assimilate them. Your life is like a TV series that has a lot of episodes, at the end of each one there's a *to be continued…* Don't get ahead of yourself. Live each one, one by one. The period that you were in the Residence you felt oppressed by your talents. Enjoy them in this life. I congratulate you, Eva. You're making good progress. We'll keep in touch. Light, love and peace."

"Thank you, master. Your return makes me feel extremely lucky. It's a great privilege."

The process that's brought me to the crystal is fascinating: the last coin that I had in my back pocket took me to the bar. In the bar I found the newspaper with the ad. The ad took me to Ric. And Ric took me to the shelter and the crystal. I think it goes back a bit further in time. Maybe someone, up there, asked: "Is there a volunteer for the crystal mission on Earth?" And I didn't think twice about raising my hand. And here I am, carrying it out, completing it, trying to finish it gracefully, all things considered.

Now I understand why Ric thanked me for accepting the translation because, deep down, I was accepting to restart my commitment as the keeper or guardian of the crystal. So many things are happening to me that in the past I would have considered incredible and now they almost seem normal. If I were to explain them to someone they would think I was crazy. When I tell Ani she won't believe me!

The Encounter

What's that noise? It sounds like an animal moving through the dead leaves! It could be a wild boar! I'll go quickly and get the shepherd's cane. Or better yet, I'll lock myself in the shelter. Those heaths are moving, over... There's something over there... What is it? I can't believe it! It's not possible. It must be an illusion, a hallucination. It's a person! This is so exciting I can't contain my impulse. I've leaped up like a spring, running desperately to reach him. I throw myself at him, almost knocking him over. I'm hugging him tightly. I've startled him. He's perplexed by my warm welcome. I'm trembling with emotion, laughing hysterically. I can't control my actions.

"Who are you? Where do you come from? Can you understand my language? What's your name? Do you live in these mountains? Are you lost? What country are you from?" Oh gosh! I'm going to try to control myself. He probably thinks I'm drunk.

"Sorry for my excitement. I've been alone for a long time and I've missed seeing people, being with people, speaking and listening to people."

"Yes, I understand."

He's confused by my warm greeting. I'm going to calm myself down. He didn't hug me back, leaving his arms by his side. He's attentively scanning my face. He looks at me, surprised. My hair must be messed up, of course, I wasn't expecting anyone. I haven't looked in a mirror since I got here. I would even scare myself!

"My name is Eva."

"Yes, I know. I'm David."

"How do you know?"

"I'm your neighbor."

"My neighbor?! I've never seen you. Have you just arrived?"

"No, when you arrived I was already here."

"Do you live far away? Is that the reason why you haven't introduced yourself as my neighbor in this desert of mountains?"

"No, that's not the reason. I live up there, on that summit, next to the three tallest trees. You can see part of my cabin. You can't see it very well because it's made out of logs and it blends into the background."

"Didn't you know? Didn't you realize that I lived down here?" I'm getting angry. "Is that the reason why you didn't come down and introduce yourself as my neighbor?"

"Yes, I knew. I could hear your voice. I could hear it from my cabin."

"Did you hear me when I went out in to the valley to scream my prayers at the Universe so that it could introduce someone to me, because I couldn't live without communicating with someone, because my loneliness was tearing me apart? Could you hear all of that? And you didn't deign to come down and tell me: 'Eva, you're not alone, I'm up there if you need me for anything.' Instead, you show up weeks after. Have you been up there all this time, knowing that I was here, without lowering yourself to come down and visit me?"

"Yes, on occasions I thought about coming down and greeting you, but..."

"But you didn't do it. You didn't make up your mind, even though you could hear my desperate plea to have someone to talk to." Wow! I really need to control myself. I'm hitting him on the chest. Anger is pushing me. The fact that he didn't come down earlier enrages me. I can't control my violence, anger, fury, the rage that I have inside is stronger than me. I've never pushed or hit anyone before. Why am I so hurt that he didn't visit me? Why am I disrespecting him as if I've known him forever?

"Leave, and it's better that you don't return. Don't treat me as if I were a charity case."

What am I saying?! He's the only person in the valley and I'm saying goodbye to him in a terrible way. It doesn't surprise me that he didn't want to come down, he feared facing the valley ogre.

"There's a reason why I didn't come down…"

"No, sorry, I don't want to hear it. There aren't any excuses. There's no other reason but lack of sensitivity. You're a person with an armored heart." I can't contain my words. I'm very angry. His rejection has irritated me, his scorn, knowing that I lived down here and he didn't deign himself to come down and introduce himself, greet me, like any good neighbor would do.

"I'm sorry, seriously, from the bottom of my heart… Goodbye."

His apology has confused me. It's dismantled my fury. It doesn't match with the arrogance and coldness that I had classified him with.

He slowly moves away. His sunken, stooped aspect moves my heart. He turns and looks at me with a long, impotent, painful expression on his face. I see the glimmer of a tear! He continues to walk away, almost as if in slow motion. I've treated him as if he didn't have feelings. I feel a strong impulse to run after him and apologize. My body doesn't respond. I can't move. What stops me? My confusion, my wounded pride, his lack of affection in not coming down and introducing himself, greeting me…?

He's wrecked. He wasn't able to overcome my fury, confront it. He was speechless, with a knot in his throat, unable to defend himself. I can't get it out of my head. Who was cruel, him or me? I didn't let him speak so that he could explain why he hadn't visited me before. I shut his mouth with unexpected abruptness. It is so embarrassing. Why didn't he come down before? There could be a thousand reasons. He might be doing some healing in the valley, trying to forget something painful, recover from something…

I treated him as if he were as hard as a rock and now I've realized that my words and my attitude have hurt him, that he's very sensitive and vulnerable.

It hurt me a lot to see him so down, seeing how sad he was as he left. His tear unleashed something that was dormant in me, I don't know what it is… When I saw how down he was because of my reprimand, I felt his pain, his sadness in my heart. When he started to leave I realized that I had made a big mistake in the way I judged him. I felt a strong urge to run after him, to apologize, to ask for forgiveness, but I dont know why I couldn't move. I should have followed my impulse and apologized for the way I treated him, for not listening to his reasons. I practice being tolerant and humble a lot but when the time comes to demonstrate it, my old attitudes and my arrogant ego come back and I unleash my claws, my thorns…

All of those readings have been pointless if when the opportunity shows up I still fill my words and gestures with bile instead of understanding, showing tolerance and love. I've spent all of this time asking for someone to talk to and when the only person in this desert of mountains shows up I ruin everything. I violently kick him out with my offensive manners.

I feel so bad for my unacceptable attitude. I feel an urgent need to go up and apologize, ask him for forgiveness for my rude manners. I've expressed myself in an awful way. It's too late now. It's getting dark. Tomorrow I'll get up early and go up to see him. It's the only way I can reconcile with him… with myself.

Why did I have that fulminating, limitless hysterical reaction? Why did it hurt me so much? I made a mistake by thinking that his silence was actually contempt, indifference, arrogance… What really exasperated me was that he knew that I was down here, but he didn't deign to visit me. Once I calmed down my wounded pride, my impolite ego, and I peacefully thought about it, my exaggerated reaction made me feel sad, remorseful, regretful and guilty. Tonight I won't be able to sleep because I'll be tossing and turning about what happened today.

I treated him like I used to treat my city friends, who had their sensibility and pride armored, and took every criticism as a joke, as a gag.

From his cabin he's heard all of my complaints, my shouts, my curses... It wasn't a view that could fascinate him and encourage him to come down.

I'm impatiently waiting for the night to be over so that I can go up and apologize. Once it's dawn and it clears up a little I'll go up. I hope there's good weather. I don't know the route, I'll leave as soon as possible so that it doesn't get dark and I don't get lost again. I'll take the backpack with the gear inside of it. I'll leave some ribbon behind, making signs... I can sense my grandma's energy!

"Hi Eva, why are you so sad?"

"Grandma! It's so nice to be able to talk to you! I'm so sad. I treated him so cruelly, grandma. I regret it so much. He'll never want to see me again, to come down."

"He appreciates you a lot and understands your reaction. He knows about your bad temper sometimes, but he also knows about your sensibility and your heart's richness. He's a beautiful being, just like you. Tomorrow you'll make up and you'll have a good relationship. Dry your tears because happiness is going to enter your heart. Today is a great day for you,. A day full of encounters."

"Why grandma?"

"Finally, Life is going to reveal to you where your sadness comes from. Today your pressing desire for it to disappear, which you've had throughout your life, will be fulfilled."

"That's great news, grandma! I can hardly believe it. It comes from a previous life, doesn't it?"

"No, from this one. It started before you were born, during your mother's pregnancy."

"Tell me, grandma. I'm very impatient."

"Someone else is going to tell you, through me. It's going to surprise you more than you can imagine. She's next to me waiting to talk to you. She's the person who you've instinctively missed the most during your life. It's your mother."

"I'm moved! Full of emotion, I can't hold back my tears. I've missed my mother so much."

"Dear Eva, my heart's daughter, we can finally communicate. I call you my daughter, because you would have liked to be called that during your childhood. However, in this space where I am, family relationships don't exist. They stay behind. We're all soulmates that find each other again and again during the course of our endless existence with different roles, sometimes as siblings, other times as parents, neighbors, enemies, friends…

Let your tears flow. They're tears of happiness. They'll dissolve the last residues of your pain and solitude. Today is going to be the happiest day of your life. Finally, you will no longer feel bitter, alone, guilty and inferior. You deserve it. You've suffered a lot. You've wanted these feelings to disappear so many times. I know that you're anxious to know what traumatized you.

I'm going to tell you why your sorrows didn't go away. Before being born, with my guides, we planned that in my next incarnation I would die after giving birth, to cancel a debt in one of my past lives. We needed a volunteer that would accept being born under those conditions. You showed up and volunteered, even though you knew it would be a heavy load to deal with in your next life.

We talked about it, accepted it and made an agreement. We completed, with the help of our guides, our next incarnation's project with the lessons and work that corresponded to us.

With this commitment you also got rid of an old debt. Your suffering was not for free, it will be good for your development.

From my maternal nest you heard your father and the doctor advise me to have an abortion. This objection to your birth nailed itself to you.

My death, my dawn in this new dimension wasn't dramatic because my seed, you, my soul's Eva, had taken root in life. It changes how you see life if you know that death is only a pause, that the soul continues to exist."

"Then, mother, my dear mother, you chose your own death. I wasn't responsible for it?"

"That's right. However, when you were born you forgot about the pact and you took on, subconsciously, the responsibility for my death. You've been carrying the weight of that guilt around since then, throughout the years. From this moment on, the knowledge of what happened liberates you from the immense feelings of isolation, blame and inferiority that you have had. From now on you're going to feel a lot lighter. Eva, we'll continue having conversations through your grandmother, until you can adjust your vibration to ours."

"Thank you, mother, I feel immensely emotional and happy. Your words have made my heart's pain and blame go away. I love you so much mother."

"Me too Eva. You have another surprise. Here, next to me, I have your father, impatiently waiting to speak to you, also through your grandmother."

I'm immensely shocked! I don't want to listen to him, I feel rejection. I can't control my crying, it's stronger than me.

"My dear Eva, I've always been with you, guiding you, helping you with what I could. I've never forgotten you. For a long time, I've wanted to communicate with you so much that now my heart explodes with happiness. My words will explain why you felt sadness and rejection when you found out that I was here.

I've always loved you, my dear daughter, even when I told your mother not to have you. The doctor warned us about the high risk that giving birth would have on her life. It was because I feared she would die, and not because I didn't love you. Your mother and I desperately wanted to have children. Don't doubt my love for you. I didn't realize that I was hurting you, all my attention was centered on the risk to your mother's life.

During the pregnancy, you heard how I tried to convince your mother not to have you, that giving birth to you could put her life at risk. You saw my objection as a lack of love toward you, which filled you with a bitterness that you've dragged along, and it's made you suffer throughout your life. I've never felt lack of affection toward you. It was the love that I had for your mother. I feared losing her more than my own life.

Her decision to give birth to you was unshakable. My continuous pleas didn't work. I gave up and accepted it.

She told me that leaving life wasn't a failure, that it was only a comma in her endless book of existence.

She considered her death as accomplishing your mission, your pact. You both evolved with the situation. Your mother accepted it when she saw that you lived. She knew that from the space where she was flying to, she could continue taking care of you, and that your grandmother would continue to be by your side giving you love. She felt that having you, even giving up her life, was worth it. It was an intuition that she heard from within her heart and she didn't doubt it.

When your mother died, my life became empty. It lost all of its meaning. I couldn't overcome it. My mental and physical pain didn't go away. An immense nostalgia invaded me, making me forget everything that didn't involve her. I left you in your grandmother's care..."

"Can you give me some proof of your love?"

"I've taken care of you since I died. I've filled your path with daisies, your favorite flower. I've sent you messengers. The daisy seller, the daisy flowerpot on the table that was in the shelter, the little yellow bird, the man in your dream who got out of the convertible..."

"It was you, father?!"

"Yes, we have resources here, with certain limits."

"Why didn't you contact me before?"

"We wanted to, but your hardships were helping you cancel some debts that you had in a past life, and you were increasing your vibration, making it possible to communicate through your grandmother. After these revelations your sorrows and your heart's regret will disappear. We'll continue to communicate. Don't forget to ask us for something when you need it. Love and light, dear Eva."

"Thank you, father, I love you a lot."

We're getting Closer...

I can't hold up my body, but I've done it. There's the cabin. It's a real traditional cabin built out of wooden logs.

It's getting worse. There's so much thunder they resound one after another. They resonate a lot. They're deafening. This curtain of water is covering the cabin. No, not again. No repetitions. I don't want to get lost again.

I'll hurry up. I can still see it, about fifty steps more, straight ahead, and I'm there. Ahhh! I've slipped. I'm sliding. The ground is inclined and it's slippery. I can't find anything to hold on to. Aaaah! I'm falling into a void. A bush has stopped me! I was able to grab on to it. Ohhh no! I'm hanging off a cliff. I won't move. I don't want to look down. Bush, please resist. Creator, help me.

"Daviid, Daaaviiiiid, help, please help me!"

I hope he's in his cabin and he hears me. It might be difficult with the storms' racket. Go away negative thoughts, I'm sure he'll hear me. I'll scream with all of my lungs' strength.

"David, Daviiiiid, Daviiid!"...

Ah, there he is!

"Hold on for a few more seconds, Eva, I'm going to go look for a rope. Don't move. Hold on tight."

He called me Eva. It sounded so nice, it's touched my heart. Hold on, bush friend, until he gets here. It has stopped raining, it's clearing up. I must look awful. Thankfully this wonderful raincoat is waterproof. It hasn't let a single drop of water get through and its kept my clothes dry. Whoever designed it deserves an ovation.

I can take off the hood. I can hold on well with one hand thanks to this rocky ledge I'm leaning my feet against. My hair is dry. Why did I worry so much about being presentable? It's the last thing I should be thinking about in this dangerous situation. Wow, he's quick, he's already coming down with a rope tied around him.

"I've tied two ropes to a strong tree to make sure we can go up safely. I've brought one for you. I'll get closer right away."

"I'll get closer right away." It reminds me of something. What is it? I have it on the tip of my tongue... The dream with the eyes! "We're getting closer." I had forgotten it. He's coming down with visible agility. He's reached me.

"I'll tie the rope safely and firmly around you."

He's passing the rope below my arms. I can feel his chest next to mine. His cheek touches my neck. It's like a hug, I can feel his warm breath on the back of my neck. I can hardly breathe...

"Sorry, I can't tie you in a different way."

"Don't worry."

He also perceives how close we are. He moves away, he stops when he sees me looking at him, his face is very close to mine, our breaths intermingle. His eyes are captivating, they fascinate me. They're the eyes from my dream!! Who are you? I have a vague feeling that I know him, that we've met before. What a magical moment! The Universe unites our auras, our energies, our chemistry. It's touching us with its strength. It wraps us with its light and sphere music. Like attracts like, it's only a matter of time... It happens so easily and spontaneously, like two clouds that find each other and become one. Wow, what an irresistible moment!

He's also fascinated by the enchantment of the moment. He's trying to move away from me. It's difficult for him to separate his energy from mine, unstring his look from mine. It's also difficult for me. "We're getting closer!" Everything has its perfect moment. He has such a deep presence, as if I've known him forever, he gives off so much tenderness, friendship and love. He's making a feeling emerge within my heart that has been sleeping for a long time.

"I'll go up first and from up there, I'll pull you up."

"I'll try to climb up on my own. Let's see how well I can do it."

"Okay, if you think that it's too difficult, tell me. If you're not used to it, it can be hard. It's a very steep wall."

"Excellent, you've done it."

"Yes, thanks to the fact that I've lost a lot of weight. Before coming to the valley I would have needed a crane... You've saved my life, David. I'm very grateful to you. I'll never forget it. From the bottom of my heart, thank you."

"Thank Life, because it takes good care of you. I'll share your thanks with the bush that stopped you from falling, with your fast reflexes that allowed you to hold on to one of its strong branches, with the rocky step you were able to lean your feet on, with the wind, because if it had blown in the opposite direction I wouldn't have heard your cry for help, with the necessity of having to go look for some firewood when you were calling me, with having a rope at hand..."

"Wow, you have the fire lit. This warmth is great. What a welcoming!"

"Eva, coming up here through a territory that you didn't know was very risky. The reason must be important."

"Yes, it is. I felt an extreme urgency to see you and apologize for my unforgivable behavior yesterday. For the disrespectful way that I treated you. When you left I felt so guilty. I'm very sorry, David. I beg you to forgive the attitude that I had yesterday. Why are you suddenly so silent?"

"The fact that you've climbed up to this high summit, putting your life in danger to apologize to me, has touched me. It means a lot to me."

"You're also healing from lack of love, is that right?"

"That's right… You've put an end to that, by coming up here and apologizing. It's touched me so deeply that it's untied the knot that has oppressed my emotional state for long time."

"I'm so happy! It's such a coincidence. Life also took away my sorrows yesterday."

"Let's celebrate it. Would you like some thyme tea sweetened with honey?"

"Great. Make sure it's very warm. This log cabin is made in the old fashioned way. It's what I expected to find in the valley instead of the strange shelter."

"Eva, would you choose the shelter or the cabin?"

"Have you been in the shelter, David?"

"Yes, I know it, it's like a toy."

"That's a good definition. Upon arrival, I would have chosen, without a doubt, the cabin, but now I'll keep the shelter. It's very special. At the beginning some things sounded miraculous to me. Later, when you coexist with 'miracles', when they become routine, we see them as being normal things. What was magical stops being magical when you find out how it works, its tricks, and its scientific explanations. It happened with the cell phone, the computer, the TV, the holographic image, the Internet… The unstoppable hordes of fantastic things that are coming out into the market are wasting away our ability to be astonished. Science has advanced a lot in the past few years."

"Wait a bit longer, Eva, it's going to be wonderful. It's already wonderful. I'm one of the biggest wonders. I went from being a microscopic and hasty spermatozoid to being an extraordinary body. However, when I look at myself in the mirror I'm not amazed, I consider myself normal and somewhat ugly."

"Ha, ha! I think you're very attractive. It's so pleasant here, with the heat from the fire, hearing the heavy rain outside."

"Do you feel like eating something?"

"Yes, of course, I haven't eaten all day."

"Today, I've made apple and corn pancakes. Maybe you'll like them."

"I'm sure I will. They look really good."

"They're easy and quick to make. My meals are tasty, simple and natural. They're warm, try one."

"What a delicious color! It's scrumptious."

There's such a pleasant relationship between us now. Who could have imagined it yesterday afternoon? I considered him unalterable, hard, distant... Today I've discovered that he's warm, human, sensitive, brave, strong, noble... First impressions are sometimes deceiving, labels that are made too quickly.

"It's curious, David, how the valley's influence has widened my perspective on things. It allows me to perceive, reflect, feel everything in more depth. My mind has calmed down, matured. My skepticism has plummeted."

"I understand. The same thing has happened to me."

"The city's rhythm made me turn like a spinning-top with the same old topics. When I first got here, the change was fierce. It was very intense and very difficult for me."

"Yes, Eva, I know."

"You know?"

"The wind brought the troubles that you told the Universe close to me. The echo spread your words throughout the mountains. I received them while I was walking, cooking... your hardships nailed themselves onto my heart."

"Oh no! Please don't tell me that the echo took my complaints to the mountains. As far as I can see, I didn't only open up my heart to the stars, but also to you. Surely every time you heard my shouting you thought, "There's that scandalous valley woman again, affecting my peace, and that of the mountains, with her screaming". Even thinking about it makes me feel embarrassed."

"Eva, you're going to be surprised with what I'm going to tell you. Your moaning, which came from your soul's states, your torn complaints full of deep sadness, your requests thrown at space with a cracked voice, the rage you had because you couldn't get rid of your sorrows, gave off a sign that you had an old pain nailed to your heart that made you suffer.

I realized that I wasn't the only one who was going through some tough times. I wanted to go down and see if I could ease your solitude. Then I reflected, and I decided that only you could conquer it. It was a face to face fight between you and it. If I had come down and interfered I could have blocked the process. Life had facilitated you with a healing silence so that you could overcome your pain and I had to respect that.

Your complaints liberated me from being lost in the thoughts that I was submerged in. Your words, the pain in your broken voice, were like a medicine for me. They woke me up from a sad and long dream.

The way you emptied your hardships from your heart showed me how to empty mine, which were compressed inside of me for a long time. You threw them out with force and rage, I kept them inside, without tears, without complaints, without asking for help. They were hurting me.

I was trapped in a silence, in an inertia that didn't let me move forward. You came out when you couldn't take it anymore and then your contained anger exploded. You bellowed it as a plea for help. You fought, you raved and you proclaimed your protests, pushed by the lonely feeling that burdened your heart. And then you gave up and you dropped to your knees, asking for help.

Your clamors towards the Heavens didn't make me reject you. I understood that it was your escape valve for something that was causing you a lot of harm. On the contrary, your voice brought me closer to a suffering being, who couldn't stand her lacerating pain, caused by an immense feeling of loneliness. I used them as a mirror. I realized that my pain wasn't the only one that existed, that I was increasing it by looking at it with a magnifying glass. Your arrival has only given me blessings. Coming up to apologize, even at the cost of losing your life, has shaken me from top to bottom. It's freed me from my old chain. It has woken me up, helping me to reconcile with life. I wanted to thank you for your help. Your attitude has helped me a lot."

"What you're saying makes me so glad. My idea about how you perceived my complaints was so different."

"This whole time I've been keeping an eye out for you, just in case you needed something or if you had a setback and you required my help. I followed your tracks to where they ended at the cave's wall. I sat down to rest for awhile and afterwards I continued looking for you. I fell asleep. The noise that the landslide made woke me up. I witnessed your spectacular escape from the cave, how you ran out wrapped around a great dust cloud, without having suffered any damage.

I sighed deeply and thanked the Heavens for having saved your life. My heart pounded quickly. I was fascinated by your astonishing flight and at the same time happy that you were safe and sound. I started to move up toward the cabin. I thought it was best not to interrupt your self-recognition process. Nevertheless, I must admit that I had a tremendous desire to find out what your adventure had been like."

"I'm so touched by your concern, your pursuit in wanting to know how I was… and I thought I was alone. Thank you for respecting the fact that I had to face my hardships alone. They were my lessons. I've been able to overcome them and they've made me stronger."

"Did we come to Earth in order to learn lessons, Eva?"

"I think so, to keep developing, the idea is to leave better than how we came, with more wisdom, with a wider consciousness."

"What do you know about spiritual topics, Eva?"

"Not a lot. Just what I got from my grandmother's books, my emotional ups and downs, my dreams and my experiences in the valley."

"We're in a magical world. How can you explain the light that radiates from the shelter's walls, the screen where you can order things and how the supplies get to the shelter?"

"Yes, David, they're dream-like. They're technologies that are far more advanced than the current ones, but there you have them. It's incredible that they were carried out long ago by a more scientifically advanced civilization than ours, and that they still work. I don't know how, just like a lot of today's technology. It helps me and I use it gratefully. I'm surprised by the prodigies we've achieved since we climbed down from the trees. Why are you smiling, David?"

"Because of your fine irony full of philosophy. I would stay up all night listening to you, Eva. Speaking to you is fascinating, but you're falling asleep."

"Yes, my eyes are closing. I can't control them."

"You can use the bed. It's very comfortable. I'm used to sleeping on the floor. I've spent most of my life living in the mountains."

"Good morning, Eva, have you rested?"

"Good and radiant morning, David, I slept wonderfully. What about you? I feel bad that you had to sleep on the floor."

"My body can't tell the difference. I don't sleep much. I got up early to do my meditation session and a few yoga postures. Do you practice meditation, Eva?"

"Yes, at first it was really difficult. I had problems starting. Now it gives me joy, each time more and more, as I learn how to dominate it. What does meditation mean to you, David?"

"A mind training practice, with which you're able to quiet it down, lower it to your heart, free of thoughts. I think that any activity done during the day becomes a slight meditation practice, if you focus your attention on it, trying not to stray away from it by letting other ideas interfere with what's at work. It's not as intense as when you quietly sit down to meditate exclusively, but it has its validity. It strengthens your mental concentration. I think that meditation pacifies us. It allows us to receive those ideas that life reserved for us, and that it couldn't give to us because it found our mental mailbox overflowing with thoughts, without any free space to put them."

"What's that noise? It sounds like an engine!"

"It's Ricard with his helicopter. He brought me here with it."

"Ric's flying a helicopter! That's the last thing I would've imagined. There he is! It's so surprising, I'm speechless! He doesn't have anywhere to land."

"Hi, Eva, can you hear me over the engine and propellers' noise?"

"Yes, I can hear you. Hi, Ric, I really wanted to see you, I'm so happy."

"I'm really glad to see you too, Eva. How are you, David?"

"Good. Nice to see you, Ricard."

"You both look really good, weather-beaten by the air, sun and Mother Earth's energy, there's nothing like the outdoor life."

"Are you coming to pick me up, Ric?"

"Yes, Eva, is that okay?"

"… Yes, Ric, no problem."

"I'll toss you a small ladder. Will you be able to climb it?"

"I'll hold on to it with my teeth if I have to."

The propellers strong wind has unbuttoned David's shirt. He has three marks on his chest, close to his heart. They're in the same place as…! Yes, I'm positive. Their location coincides with the arrows that were nailed in my love's chest during that past life. I'm delirious! It's impossible! It's him!! It's thrilling. It's been such a long time. From the beginning. Two halves that fit together, that perfectly coincide, that are one.

"You're surprised by my marks. They're birthmarks."

"Do they hurt like as if you had something nailed there?"

"Yes, sometimes. How do you know that?"

"It's a long story. It's very important. I'll tell you some other time. I'll write my address and telephone number on this paper for you. If you want you can stay in my house, I have a spare room that you could use. I'll be extremely happy if you accept."

"Thank you, Eva, of course I accept. I want to from the bottom of my heart."

"Do you know when you'll return to the city?"

"As soon as possible. I'll ask Ricard."

"Ricard, when can you take me back?"

"How about tomorrow, David?"

"Perfect. What time should we leave?"

"What about four o'clock in the afternoon? Will you have time to organize everything?"

"Yes, I should have enough time."

"Eva, can David pick up your things and take them to you tomorrow? That way we don't have to land in the shelter?"

"Yes, I only have a suitcase and a backpack."

"Is that okay with you, David?"

"No problem, Ricard."

"See you tomorrow, Eva. I'm curious to know what the marks are. You're crying."

"It's going to surprise you. You can't even imagine it. I'll give you a clue so that you can start thinking about it: Hello, scribe."

"Hello, scribe! These words have activated my historical memory. Crystal guardian! Yes, time has passed! "In less than a butterfly's flutter, we'll be together again, in another life". Do you remember? We've finally found each other during the time of the prodigies. My love."

"You've just confirmed that they weren't just things I was inventing. I feel so happy. Can you give me your hand?"

"Why are you writing your address on my hand?"

"Just in case the paper flies away."

"Don't be afraid, Life has driven us on this long trip without getting us lost."

"Sometimes Life uses us as assistants."

"Yes, it divides up the work."

"Give me a hug, David, let's join our hearts…"

"I feel the same energies from back then! Do you remember them, Eva?"

"Yes, we'll keep on increasing them. We'll love each other in our hearts' light."

"No dark fortified Residence."

"I don't even want to think about it."

The Return

"You've climbed up with a monkey's agility, Eva."

"It's all the practicing that I did in the valley. I didn't stop going up and down…"

"Okay, let's go. Have you ever flown in a helicopter, Eva?"

"I haven't been in a helicopter or an airplane, or even a hot-air balloon."

"How was your stay in the valley? From what I've seen, it was first-class."

"There was a lot of action Ric, you can't even imagine it! Life has beaten me up a lot, and it has woken me up. I'm very grateful to you. Thanks for this unusual holiday."

"You have to thank yourself, it was something you wanted, your inner desire, your plan that brought you here."

"Ric, I had so many questions to ask you, and now my mind is blank."

What a gigantic landscape! A wavy green cover of enormous trees as far as I can see. I'm leaving behind so many memories here, so much emotion, so many experiences that have made me mature. Tomorrow my little yellow bird, my squirrel friend, my chatterbox parrot, my monkey friends and the pleasant butterfly will miss me. I won't forget you, you'll always be in my heart. Someday I'll come back to say hello. Dear scribe, extraordinary scribe… Life, you're so magical, you've brought us together again.

"You're so quiet, Eva. You're crying."

"Yes, they're tears of happiness for the encounters, and tears of sadness for the farewells. I'm leaving behind so many things here, distancing myself from those I love, who've traveled with me along different paths, not feeling them next to me. This is such a massive ocean of mountains. It's endless. It looks like a green tide. Where are we, Ric? Don't answer, no more questions, knowing that it's a magnificent place where I've had intense experiences is enough for me. They've widened my consciousness. They've taken away my sorrows. They've made so many desired encounters and so many other things possible…"

Everything is coming together, taking shape. I've come to these places in order to resume my mission, to recover the stars' legacy. My past indecisiveness has allowed my mind to become more open, neutral, free, perceptive, humble, clear, strong…

"Ric, do you understand the Creator's magic?"

"I've been chasing it for a long time. He gave me eternity and told me… look for Me. And I began the search. He put a compass with His Light in my heart so that I wouldn't get disorientated. He's so Immeasurable! It's like if you're flying a spaceship, the fastest one, in a straight line, and you see how fast the stars pass beside it and stay behind. You think that someday there won't be anymore and that another thing will start, but you advance a million years and the stars, the worlds, continue rapidly sliding, and such infinity overwhelms you, makes you shudder. An unrestrainable emotion emerges within you. Do you understand what I'm trying to explain to you, Eva?"

"Yes, Ric, sometimes, when I look up at the sky with its endless amount of stars I begin to shiver. I cannot comprehend such magnitude so I cover myself with humility and I lean on the Light I have inside of me that points toward Him, and I ask it to guide me."

"I'm falling asleep. I'm tired from yesterday, going up to David's cabin. I'm exhausted, sleepy, my eyes are closing. I can't control them. I was very interested in what you were telling me. It sounded so lovely Ric. You're fantastic."

Mountains, mountains, mountains… I thought that I wouldn't find neighbors here… and I had him next to me. My love… Life has brought us together again, I've missed you so much… without knowing it… It's so calming… I'm so sleepy… so drowsy… I'm so weightless… I'm falling asleep… My soul's Scribe… immensely loved… since the beginning… It was worth it… waiting… for the butterflies flutter…

"Eva, wake up. We're here."

What? Where am I? It's nighttime. It's the fountain in the square. I'm in front of my house! In the helicopter with Ric. How did he know my address? He's landed in the middle of the square! He can't park a helicopter in a public place, just like that. He's calmly looking at me.

"Did you have good dreams, Eva?"

I have an intuition. Ric is the Residence's architect! I'm going to ask him. He looks at me smiling, he's received my question through a mental email.

"Say my name backwards and what do you get?"

"Of course! Ric backwards is Cir. How didn't I get the clue before? Time has joined our paths again. Over there, in the distance, there's a police car. Take off before they get here so that you don't have any problems. Have a hug. Take care, Ric. I love you very much."

"I love you, too. We'll stay in touch. You're forgetting this envelope. It's your salary."

"Wow! I forgot about the payment!"

I quickly run off, I'm close to the house's entrance. Ric is gone. He's taken off very quickly, I didn't even realize it. Here comes the police car. They open the car's door and get out, I don't think they've seen me.

"Hey, you, stop!"

Oh no, how am I going to get out of this one?

"Yes, officer." They're astonished, looking at the place where just a moment ago the helicopter had been.

"Have you seen a helicopter?"

"A helicopter! Here? Where is it?" I look at them suspiciously, as if they were talking nonsense, like drunks.

"It was here a moment ago, in the middle of the square."

"Officer, are you serious? You probably saw some street lights or a bright ad's reflection in the window displays. A helicopter wouldn't be able to land and take off without its propellers cutting off some of the branches of the trees. Do you see any on the ground?" Wow, Ric, that's true. How did you do it?

"That's right, Miss, there's not a single branch on the ground. It was probably a reflection. Maybe it came from the police car's windshield."

They're confused, I made them doubt themselves. I've taken control of the situation.

"Thank you Miss, goodnight and sorry."

"Goodnight officers, have a good shift."

Thankfully they believed everything that I said to them. The last thing I needed, at this time of the day, was to be taken to the police station and interrogated. I'm falling asleep. Your dance was so quick, Time friend. It seems like it was only yesterday when I left to go to The Four-Leaf Clover.

What a big leap in time! Cir, the Residence's architect, my dear Scribe and I, the three of us riding together again! What a magical Universe!